First Edition

biography for beginners

African-American Leaders, Volume 2

Actors, Artists, Authors, Dancers, Musicians, and Entrepreneurs

Laurie Lanzen Harris,
Editor

Favorable Impressions

P.O. Box 69018 • Pleasant Ridge, MI 48069

Laurie Lanzen Harris, *Editor*
Laurie Collier Hillstrom,
Claire A. Rewold, PhD, *Contributing Editors*
Dan R. Harris, *Senior Vice President, Sales and Marketing*

The Library of Congress has catalogued the
combined volume edition as follows:

Library of Congress Cataloging-in-Publication Data
Biography for beginners : African-American leaders / Laurie Lanzen Harris, editor.
p. cm.
Includes bibliographical references and index.
ISBN 978-1-931360-35-7 (alk. paper)
ISBN 978-1-931360-36-4 (v.2)
1. African Americans—Biography—Dictionaries, Juvenile. 2. Successful people—United States—Biography—Dictionaries, Juvenile. 3. African American leadership—Dictionaries, Juvenile. I. Harris, Laurie Lanzen. II. Title: African-American Leaders.
E185.96.B475 2007
902′.009296073—dc22
[B] 2007041045

ISBN-13 978-1-931360-36-4

This book is printed on acid-free paper meeting the ANSI Z39.48 Standard. The infinity symbol that appears above indicate that the paper in this book meets that standard.

Printed in the United States

Contents

Preface

Welcome to *Biography for Beginners: African-American Leaders, Volume 2.* This is the second of a two-volume series and covers African-American actors, artists, authors, dancers, musicians, and entrepreneurs. Volume 1 in the series features profiles of civil rights, political, and social leaders; scientists and inventors; and athletes.

Since beginning the *Biography for Beginners* series in 1995, we have published four monographs in areas of high interest for young readers, including U.S. Presidents, world explorers, authors, and inventors. Several years ago we surveyed librarians for additional areas of interest for young readers, and they suggested African-American leaders.

The Plan of the Work

Like *Biography for Beginners: Presidents of the United States, World Explorers*, and *Inventors, African-American Leaders* is written for early readers, ages 7 to 10. The volume is especially created for young students in a format they can read, understand, and use for assignments. The entries are arranged alphabetically. Each entry begins with a heading listing the individual's name, birth and death dates, and a brief description of his or her importance to the history of African-American achievement. Boldfaced headings lead readers to information on birth, youth, growing up, education, marriage and family, and the nature of the individual's accomplishment.

Entries end with a list of World Wide Web sites. These sites have been reviewed for accuracy and suitability for use by young students. A bibliography of works used in the compilation of the entries is at the end of the Preface.

The entries also include portraits of the individual, as well as paintings, photos, and other illustrations to enhance the reader's understanding of the person's achievement.

Audience

This book is intended for young readers in grades two through five who are studying African-American history for the first time. Most children will use this book to study one individual at a time, usually as part of a class assignment. Within the entries, the names of other individuals who appear in the volume are bold-faced, to act as a cross-reference. A Glossary of terms common to Black American history appears at the end of the book. These Glossary terms appear in the text in bold-faced capitals. This section also includes brief biographies of people important to African-American history, who do not have full-length entries in the volume.

Index

An Index covering names, occupations, and key words concludes the volume. The Index has been created with the young reader in mind, and therefore contains a limited number of terms that have been simplified for ease of research.

Our Advisors

Biography for Beginners: African-American Leaders was reviewed by an Advisory Board that includes school librarians and public librarians. The thoughtful comments and suggestions of all the Board members have been invaluable in developing this publication. Any errors, however, are mine alone. I would like to list the members of the Advisory Board and to thank them again for their efforts.

Nina Levine	Blue Mountain Middle School Cortlandt Manor, NY
Nancy Margolin	McDougle Elementary School Chapel Hill, NC
Deb Rothaug	Pasadena Elementary School Plainview, NY
Laurie Scott	Farmington Hills Community Library Farmington Hills, MI
Joyce Siler	Westridge Elementary School Kansas City, MO

Your Comments Are Welcome

Our goal is to provide accurate, accessible biographical information for early readers. Please write or call me with your comments.

Acknowledgments

I would like to thank the staffs of the organizations who provided photos and illustrations for the volume, as well as the Library of Congress. Thank you to Sans Serif for outstanding design and layout.

Bibliography

This is a listing of works used in the compilation of the biographical profiles. Most of the works cited here are written at the middle school or high school reading level and are generally beyond the reading level of early elementary students. However, many librarians consider these reliable, objective points of departure for further research.

Columbia Encyclopedia, 2005 ed.
Compton's Encyclopedia, 2006 ed.
World Book Encyclopedia, 2006 ed.

Laurie Harris, Editor and Publisher
Favorable Impressions

Introduction

As in the first volume of *Biography for Beginners: African-American Leaders,* the men and women profiled in this volume have distinguished themselves in many areas of achievement: as actors, artists, authors, dancers, musicians, and entrepreneurs. What unites them is their African-American heritage, a heritage that includes the brutal history of slavery, racism, and the fight for equality and freedom. It is not the purpose of this volume to simply outline the struggles faced by these individuals. Rather, it is to celebrate their achievements, and to show how they brought about change in each of their areas of accomplishment.

Actors

The actors profiled in this volume have gained their fame in the theater, in film, and on television. Two of the greatest actors of their generation, **Ossie Davis** and **Ruby Dee,** were also activists in the struggle for Civil Rights. They formed a partnership devoted to their craft, equality, and each other. Appearing with Ruby Dee in the premiere of **Lorraine Hansberry's** *A Raisin in the Sun*, was a young actor named **Sidney Poitier**. He would go on to become the first African-American actor to win an Academy Award for Best Actor. In the 1960s, **Bill Cosby** became the first black actor to star in a TV series. By the 1980s, his family comedy, "The Cosby Show," was the top-rated show in the country. **Denzel Washington** is one of the finest actors of his generation. He has appeared on stage and in film, playing characters from Shakespeare to the films of **Spike Lee**. He won his first Oscar, for Best Actor in a Supporting Role, in 1990, for *Glory.* In 2002, he became the first African-American since Poitier to win the Oscar for Best Actor. That same year, **Halle Berry** became the first African-American woman to win the Academy Award for Best Actress. **Spike Lee's** films are vivid evocations of many problems of racism in America, from biographical films of the fiery Malcolm X, to documentaries on the devastation of Hurricane Katrina.

Artists

The artists profiled here created works inspired by the Harlem Renaissance. **Jacob Lawrence** created vivid murals depicting African-American life, including scenes of life in Harlem, and celebrating black heroes, like Frederick Douglass. **Romare Bearden** was influenced by the flowering of African-American art in Harlem, too. In a wide range of genres, from collage to watercolor to oil painting, he, too, celebrated the lives of black Americans, in Harlem and in the South. He created scenes and sets for other genres, too, including **Alvin Ailey's** dance company. **Gordon Parks** was an outstanding photographer, whose moving pictures reflect African-American life, lending dignity to those who labor and struggle, and celebrating outstanding artists like **Louis Armstrong** and **Langston Hughes.**

Authors

The group of African-American authors profiled here begins with **Phillis Wheatley**. Born in Africa, and brought to Massachusetts as a slave, she became the first African-American poet to have a book published in this country. **Paul Laurence Dunbar** wrote poems that celebrated African-American experience and culture. **Langston Hughes** is best known as a poet of the Harlem Renaissance, but he also wrote novels, plays, and short stories. His poem, *Harlem,* asks a question that has echoed down the years: "What happens to a dream deferred?" One of its most famous lines, "Does it dry up, Like a raisin in the sun?" gave **Lorraine Hansberry** the title for her famous play. First performed on Broadway in 1959, *A Raisin in the Sun* is still produced around the country.

Zora Neale Hurston was, like Hughes, a voice of the Harlem Renaissance. Virtually unknown when she died, Hurston has enjoyed a recent revival, based on the television adaptation of *Their Eyes Were Watching God*, starring **Halle Berry** and produced by **Oprah Winfrey. Ralph Ellison's** *Invisible Man* gave voice to a generation of African-Americans rendered "invisible" by racism. **Richard Wright** wrote searing indictments of racism in America, most notably in *Native Son* and *Black Boy*. **James Baldwin**, influenced and encouraged by Wright, wrote several landmark works of fiction and nonfiction that exposed the savage inequalities faced by African-Americans.

Alex Haley detailed the horrors of slavery, and the dignity and humanity of his own family background in *Roots*. The work became an international sensation, and the book's title became a synonym for the exploration of one's heritage. **Maya Angelou**, writer, dancer, performer, and activist, has incorporated the struggle for Civil Rights and the African-American experience in her poetry and prose for young and old readers alike. And **Toni Morrison**, creator of some of the finest novels of the modern era, won the Nobel Prize in Literature for a body of work that is devoted to an unflinching look at the scourge of racism on African-American life.

Among these writers are some of the finest children's authors of the era. **Virginia Hamilton** wrote many award-winning books for elementary and young adult readers that focused African-American life and folklore. **Jerry Pinkney**, who illustrated some of Hamilton's finest works, is acknowledged as one of the finest illustrators of the modern era. **Walter Dean Myers** often depicts African-American life in his picture books for young readers, as well as serious works for teenaged readers. **Christopher Paul Curtis** is one of the finest authors for middle grade readers writing now. His award-winning books feature young African-American characters, from the 19th century to the present, confronting and understanding their history.

Dancers

The four dancers profiled here span nearly 100 years of performance. **Bill "Bojangles" Robinson** began performing during Vaudeville, and brought important innovations to tap. **Alvin Ailey** was a giant in the dance world, creating one of the finest dance companies, and choreographing some of the most memorable dances of the modern era. **Judith Jamison** had a brilliant career as one of Ailey's most famous dancers, and now directs the company. **Savion Glover** has brought an entire new generation of young people to the excitement of dance.

Musicians

The musicians in this volume cover the spectrum of accomplishment, from classical music to jazz to rhythm and blues. **Marian Anderson**'s career spanned four decades, as a star of the opera and classical music stage. She also became a legendary figure in the fight for equality when, denied the right to perform at Constitution Hall in Washington, D.C. because of her race, she performed a concert on the steps of the Lincoln Memorial. **Paul Robeson** was an outstanding singer, actor, and activist, whose political beliefs led to the collapse of his brilliant career.

The jazz era was defined by two giants of 20th-century music, **Louis Armstrong** and **Duke Ellington.** As a performer, composer, and bandleader, Armstrong expanded the jazz form, creating new directions followed by jazz musicians for decades. Considered one of the finest composers of the 20th century, Ellington incorporated his African-American heritage in every part of his music. **Ella Fitzgerald,** the "First Lady of Song," performed with both of these jazz masters, and on her own as one of the finest interpreters of vocal music ever. **Miles Davis**, trumpeter and composer, developed "cool" jazz, from the rhythms and chords of bebop, transforming the art. **Wynton Marsalis** continues to perform, compose, and promote jazz music in concerts and programs at Lincoln Center and around the world.

Throughout his long career, **Ray Charles** brought about a transformation music, blending gospel, blues, jazz, and rock. In Detroit, **Berry Gordy Jr.** created the Motown Sound, featuring the talents of great singers like **Marvin Gaye** in music that blended rhythm and blues with funk and rock.

Entrepreneurs

Madam C.J. Walker became the first woman self-made millionaire, which she achieved against incredible odds. She started a successful business at a time when careers were not yet open to African-Americans or women, and helped launch the entire industry of black hair-care and cosmetic products. **Berry Gordy** began Motown as a music label, and oversaw its growth into an entertainment empire. **Oprah Winfrey** is one of the most successful businesswomen in American history. An actress, television show host, magazine publisher, and producer, she represents the best in the entrpreneurial spirit, encouraging her viewers and readers to achieve all they can be.

Laurie Harris, Editor and Publisher
Favorable Impressions

Alvin Ailey

1931 - 1989

African-American Dancer and Choreographer
Founder of the Alvin Ailey American Dance Theater

ALVIN AILEY WAS BORN on January 5, 1931, in his grandfather's cabin in Rogers, Texas. His parents were Alvin and Lula Ailey. In a small town not far from Waco, Alvin lived his early years in a small overcrowded house with thirteen people—his grandfather, parents, aunt, and eight cousins. His father left the family when Alvin was about one year old.

ALVIN AILEY GREW UP living in town after town as his mother worked as a maid to support them. In his early years, Alvin and his mother moved to Navasota, Texas, where his mother worked in a hospital.

ALVIN AILEY WENT TO SCHOOL in Navasota for elementary school and junior high. In 1942 he and his mother moved to Los Angeles. In L.A., Alvin attended Thomas Jefferson High School. He was an "A" student.

As a boy, Alvin loved to read. He was also a fluent speaker of Spanish, learned in his early years in Texas. At school he enjoyed sports and was involved in gymnastics and football. At one time he also took tap dancing lessons but he had no plan to become a dancer.

Ailey in a photo from 1955.

INTRODUCTION TO DANCE: Alvin's first introduction to dance came when he saw a performance of the Ballet Russe de Monte Carlo as a young person. That was an important early ballet company.

When he was in high school, he saw his neighbor and classmate, Carmen de Lavallade, dance during a school assembly. He was afraid of being called a "sissy," so he didn't tell anyone how much her dancing had impressed him. But one day after watching Alvin perform gymnastics, Carmen suggested that he study dance with Lester Horton, her dance teacher.

After a few dance lessons, Mr. Horton asked Alvin to rehearse with Carmen, who was his leading dancer. They were a great team from the beginning and remained close friends for the rest of their lives. He said that, "Dance, for me, would have been impossible without Carmen de Lavallade."

THE COLLEGE YEARS: Although dance was very important to Ailey, his family wanted him to go to college. He enrolled at the University of California at Los Angeles (UCLA) where he studied literature.

During college, Ailey continued to study dance at night with Lester Horton. Eventually, Ailey left college without graduating and moved to San Francisco.

LIFE IN SAN FRANCISCO: Borrowing $50 from a friend, Ailey lived in cheap hotels and the YMCA. He danced in a San Francisco night-club but didn't make much money. He enrolled in San Francisco State College and took odd jobs to pay the tuition.

It wasn't long before he missed dancing. He began going to the Halprin Lathrope Dance Studio where he met a black woman named Marguerite Angelos. She would later become known as **Maya Angelou.** They rehearsed together on weekends. Ailey began to try his hand at choreography, or creating dances.

With a group from this studio, Ailey returned to Los Angeles to dance at a benefit performance. He visited the Horton Studio and had a talk with his former teacher. Horton convinced Ailey to quit

Ailey company performing Revelations.

school and study dance. He did, and soon traveled to New York City to dance with Horton's company.

BECOMING A STAR: Ailey joined the company as his old friend Carmen de Lavallade became a star with the Horton Dance Theater. When Ailey and de Lavallade had the chance to dance together they were an immediate success. Then, tragically, Lester Horton died of a heart attack.

Aailey took over the position of choreographer and artistic director of the Horton Dance Theater. But the reviews of his first two ballet productions were not good; eventually the company broke up.

DANCING IN NEW YORK: Soon, Ailey and de Lavallade were invited to dance in the Broadway production of *House of Flowers,* a musical based on a book by Truman Capote. While he was performing in this production Ailey began to study dance at the Martha Graham school. Graham was one of the pioneers of modern dance and a legendary choreographer. She, and the African-American dancer/choreographer Katherine Dunham were important influences on him.

From the mid-1950s through the early 1960s Ailey danced in many theatrical and musical productions both on- and off-Broadway. He also had acting parts in several plays.

FOUNDING A DANCE COMPANY: In New York in the late 1950s, Ailey and another dancer put together a troupe of 35 dancers. They performed several shows at the 92nd Street YMCA. The audiences there encouraged them. That group of dancers would form the core of the Alvin Ailey American Dance Theater, founded in 1958.

EARLY WORKS OF ALVIN AILEY: Ailey's first major choreographed piece was based on blues music. *Blues Suite*, created in 1958, featured 13 men and 11 women moving in patterns across the floor. From the beginning, Ailey's dancers were an integrated troupe. They were black, white, and Asian, and they were all extraordinary.

Another early piece choreographed by Ailey turned out to be his most famous. *Revelations* was about African-American religious life. It was choreographed to black spirituals. Through this work Ailey was able to express the faith, hope, and joy of the African-American church, celebrating its choirs, congregations, and preachers. The work is still one of the most popular pieces performed by the company.

SUCCESS FOR THE ALVIN AILEY AMERICAN DANCE THEATER: During the 1960s Ailey's company performed in New York, Boston, other major cities. In 1962, with Carmen de Lavallade as co-director, the troupe performed for 13 weeks in Australia, Southeast Asia and Brazil. This tour was made possible by a grant from the U. S. Department of State. It was part of President John F. Kennedy's International Exchange Program. This was the first time a black dance company had toured Southeast Asia. They were very well received.

In 1965, the company included **Judith Jamison**, the most famous African-American soloist of modern dance. Her performance in *Cry,* Ailey's piece that celebrates black women everywhere, made it one of the troupe's best known pieces.

Ailey's company toured Europe and Africa in the late 1960s. In 1970 they performed in Russia. They were the first modern dance company to perform in the Soviet Union since the 1920s. One audience in Leningrad gave them a 23-minute standing ovation.

In the late 1960s, Ailey created another major work, *Masekela Lounge*. It is set to the music of South African activist Hugh Masekela. It is a cry from the heart about the evils of racism wherever it exists.

In the early 1970s, Ailey choreographed a work to music by the great **Duke Ellington**. Called *The River*, it is still a popular piece.

By the late 1970s the Alvin Ailey Company was one of the most popular modern dance troupes in America. They continued to tour

Ailey dancers performing at his funeral, December 8, 1989.

the world. Ailey created ballets for other companies, too, including the American Ballet Theater, the Royal Danish Ballet, the London Festival Ballet, the Joffrey Ballet, and the Paris Opera Ballet.

FINANCIAL PROBLEMS: Despite their popularity, the troupe was often in financial trouble as they scrambled to find all the money necessary to rent space, pay dancers, and pay production and touring expenses. The group would sometimes have to disband for lack of money.

LATER YEARS: Even though he was a professional success, Ailey had a troubled personal life. Over the years he developed a drinking problem and abused drugs and diet pills. In 1980 he suffered a mental breakdown and was hospitalized for seven weeks. After his release, he returned to work and produced *Phases*, his last original work.

Ailey died in New York City on December 1, 1989, of AIDS-related ailments. His funeral was attended by thousands. Two weeks after his death, **Judith Jamison** became director of the company.

ALVIN AILEY'S HOME AND FAMILY: Ailey never married or had children. He lived in New York City for most of his adult life.

HIS LEGACY: Alvin Ailey was a pioneer in the world of modern dance. The themes of his dances were often drawn from the African-American experience. They reflect the influence of ballet, modern, and Broadway dancing technique. In works like *Revelations*, he created dances that were heartfelt, exuberant, and lovingly dedicated to his African-American heritage. He also created summer camps to reach poor children and introduce them to the wonder of the arts, and of course, to dance. These continue to this day.

WORLD WIDE WEB SITES:

http://www.alvinailey.org/
http://www.pbs.org/wnet/freetodance/biographies/ailey.html

Marian Anderson

1897 - 1993

African-American Classical, Opera, and Spiritual Singer
First African-American to Perform with the Metropolitan Opera

MARIAN ANDERSON WAS BORN on February 17, 1897, in Philadelphia, Pennsylvania. Her parents were John and Anna Anderson. John sold ice and coal. Anna was a teacher before she had children. Marian was the oldest of three girls. Her two younger sisters were named Alyce and Ethel.

MARIAN ANDERSON GREW UP in a loving, nurturing home. She grew up loving music, and started to sing at three. She remembered "beating out some sort of rhythm with my hands and feet and la-la-la-ing a vocal accompaniment. Some people might say that these were the first signs of music in me. I would only say that I felt cozy and happy."

Marian's family attended the Union Baptist Church in Philadelphia. She began to sing in the church choir at age six. When she was eight, she earned her first fee. She was paid 50 cents to sing at church. Flyers circulated in the neighborhood, saying: "Come and hear the baby contralto."

"Contralto" refers to a particular range in the signing voice. There are four parts in traditional vocal music. They are soprano, alto, tenor, and bass. In her career, Marian sang as a contralto, which is between alto and tenor.

Yet, even as a child, Anderson could sing higher and lower than the traditional contralto range. She could sing an incredible three full octaves. That's 24 notes in sequence, from lowest to highest pitch. By the time she was 13, she was singing in the adult choir. If any of the soloists in any voice part couldn't perform, Marian would sing the part.

She played instruments, too. She studied piano, and, after scrubbing steps for five cents, she saved enough to buy a violin for $3.98. She played it until it fell apart.

A FAMILY TRAGEDY: When Marian was just 12 years old, her beloved father died of a brain tumor. The family had to move in with her father's parents. It was a difficult time. Anderson recalled feeling that "tragedy had moved into our house." Her grandmother was strong-willed and domineering. She was "used to being the boss of her own house and the people in it," Anderson wrote later.

Her mother went to work as a domestic laborer, and also took in laundry. Marian and her sisters helped out any way they could. Anderson was devoted to her mother. She credited her mother with giving her the strength to face all the challenges of life.

MARIAN ANDERSON WENT TO SCHOOL at the local public schools in Philadelphia. She did well in school, and remembered liking spelling bees and speech classes. She started high school at William Penn High, a commercial high school. She took typing and shorthand, courses designed to help her find an office job.

But the focus of her schooling soon changed. She sang a solo at a school concert, and an important community member heard her. He thought a young woman of Marian's talent should be taking college preparatory courses. He also thought she should be studying music. Anderson transferred to South Philadelphia High School. There, she began taking more challenging courses and studying music.

FACING RACISM: When she was 15, Anderson first faced the racist attitudes that frequently threatened her career. She tried to apply to a music school, but was rejected. "We don't take colored," the school clerk told her.

The words stung. "It was my first contact with the blunt, brutal words. This school of music was the last place I expected to hear them. True enough, my skin was different, but not my feelings." As she would do throughout her career, Anderson refused to let the bigoted views of others define her.

SERIOUS TRAINING: Anderson first began to study music seriously at 15. A well-known singer and teacher named Mary

Anderson performing on the steps of the Lincoln Memorial, April 9, 1939.

Patterson accepted her as a student, and her vocal training began in earnest.

Serious vocal training begins with developing technique. Anderson learned how to breathe properly. She did scale studies and other exercises to develop the strength and flexibility of her voice. She studied the correct pronunciations of words from several languages—English, German, French, and Latin.

Anderson loved the training, and worked hard. She knew she needed the foundation of solid technique. "The purpose of all the exercises and labors was to give you a thoroughly reliable foundation and to make sure you could do your job under any circumstances. There is no shortcut," she said.

STARTING A CAREER IN MUSIC: Anderson began performing in the Philadelphia area while she was still in high school. When she'd get paid, she'd give most of the money to her mother. She also began to study with a well-known teacher named Giuseppe Boghetti. He helped her develop the songs and sound that made her an international star.

Anderson began to study the *lieder* (LEE-der), or songs, of great composers like Franz Schubert and Johannes Brahms. They require outstanding technique, but also emotional power. They often tell a story, and are set to folktales or poems. Anderson brought out the sensitivity and beauty at the heart of these great songs. She also performed famous arias from operas by composers like Mozart and Verdi.

She was also known for her beautiful performances of spirituals. In songs like "My Lord, What a Morning" she brought to life, and celebrated, an African-American art form.

Anderson began to tour the country. She earned enough to buy a house for her mother and sisters. In 1923, she won a vocal competition in Philadelphia. She was the first African-American ever to win the contest. In 1925, she won a national competition. Her prize was the chance to perform with the great New York Philharmonic Orchestra. Her concert was a tremendous hit.

SINGING IN EUROPE: Anderson decided to travel to Europe to study and perform. She was a sensation. While touring Finland, she met the famous classical composer Sibelius. She visited him at his home, where she sang one of his pieces. "My roof is too low for you," he exclaimed.

In Austria, the great conductor Arturo Toscanini heard her sing. "Yours is a voice such as one hears once in a hundred years!" he told her.

Anderson returned to the U.S. in triumph. She began a national tour in New York City. Her schedule was hectic: she gave up to 100 concerts each year. She became a true national treasure. She was adored for her beautiful voice and artistry, and her humble, dignified manner.

SINGING AT THE WHITE HOUSE: In 1936, First Lady Eleanor Roosevelt invited Anderson to sing at the White House. She was the first African-American to sing at the President's home.

CONSTITUTION HALL AND THE D.A.R.: In 1939, Anderson became the unlikely center of a controversy. Her manager wanted to book her at Washington D.C.'s Constitution Hall. The Hall is run by the D.A.R. (Daughters of the American Revolution). It is a conservative women's group that, in 1939, would not allow African-Americans to perform.

First Lady Eleanor Roosevelt, a member of the D.A.R. was outraged. She quit the organization. Harold Ickes, then Interior Secretary, arranged to have Anderson perform at the Lincoln Memorial. It was one of the most memorable concerts ever heard in the nation's capitol.

THE LINCOLN MEMORIAL CONCERT: On Easter Sunday, April 9, 1939, Anderson stood on the steps of the Lincoln Memorial and sang to a crowd of 75,000. Among the listeners were Supreme Court justices, members of Congress, and Civil Rights and religious leaders.

Anderson posing with African-American servicemen at the January 1943 dedication of the mural depicting her 1939 concert.

Anderson walked to the platform, closed her eyes, and began to sing "America." She sang Schubert lieder, opera arias, and closed with spirituals. A hush fell over the audience. It was, in the words of one spectator, "a silence instinctive, natural, and intense, so that you were afraid to breathe."

"What were my own feelings?" Anderson wrote later about the controversy. "I was saddened and ashamed. I was sorry for the people who had precipitated the affair. I felt that their behavior stemmed from a lack of understanding. They were not persecuting me personally or as a representative of my people so much as they were doing something that was neither sensible nor good."

FIGHTING PREJUDICE IN THE CONCERT HALL: Anderson was a private woman. "I was not designed for hand-to-hand combat," she said. But she continued to confront and overcome prejudice wherever she could. While touring the South, she came face to face with the racism that limited the lives of African-Americans. It was the time of **JIM CROW** laws. Businesses—hotels, restaurants, concert halls—could legally discriminate against black people.

But when Anderson performed in the South, she refused to allow the segregated seating that was legal under Jim Crow. At that time, African-Americans could be forced to sit in segregated, inferior areas. She insisted instead that African-Americans be able to sit in every section of a performance hall.

SINGING AT THE METROPOLITAN OPERA: Anderson broke another racial barrier in the 1950s. On January 7, 1955, she became the first African-American to perform with the Metropolitan Opera, one of the most important opera companies in the world. When she appeared on stage, the audience gave her a standing ovation, before she sang a single note.

Anderson performs at the January 1943 dedication of the mural depicting her 1939 concert.

Anderson sang at the inauguration of President Dwight D. Eisenhower in 1957. President Eisenhower asked her to become a musical ambassador for the U.S.

Anderson traveled the world, singing and bringing the beauty and dignity of her music to thousands.

Eisenhower also named her to the United Nations Human Rights Committee.

In 1961, Anderson sang at another presidential inauguration, this time for John F. Kennedy. In 1964, she began her farewell tour. She started at Constitution Hall, and finished in New York's Carnegie Hall. After she retired, she frequently appeared at charity fund raisers for organizations like the **NAACP**.

Anderson also founded a scholarship given each year to a young singer. It has helped launch the careers of such great African-American singers as Grace Bumbry.

MARIAN ANDERSON'S HOME AND FAMILY: Anderson married Orpheus Fisher in 1943. They had no children. They lived on a 100-acre farm in rural Connecticut. Fisher died in 1986. Anderson developed heart disease and moved to Portland, Oregon, to live with her nephew. She died in Portland on April 8, 1993.

HER LEGACY: Marian Anderson was one of the greatest musical artists of the 20th century. She was also a courageous figure in the struggle for equal opportunity for African-Americans. At the time of her death, the opera star Jesseye Norman paid tribute to her. "Marian Anderson was the personification of all that is wonderful, simple, pure, and majestic in the human spirit. She wore the glorious crown of her voice with the grace of an empress."

WORLD WIDE WEB SITES:

http://www.library.upenn.edu/exhibits/rbm/anderson/index.html
http://www.lkwdpl.org/wihohio/ande-mar.htm
http://www.mariananderson.org/legacy/

Maya Angelou
1928 -
African-American Poet, Autobiographer, Essayist, Activist, and Author of Books for Children and Adults

MAYA ANGELOU WAS BORN on April 4, 1928, in St. Louis, Missouri. Her name when she was born was Marguerite Annie Johnson. Her parents were Bailey and Vivian Johnson. Bailey worked in a hotel and Vivian was a nurse. Maya had an older brother named Bailey. It was Bailey who gave her the nickname "Maya," because he couldn't pronounce Marguerite.

Maya's parents divorced when she three. She and Bailey were sent to live with their grandmother in Arkansas.

MAYA ANGELOU GREW UP in the little town of Stamps, Arkansas. Her grandmother was named Annie Henderson, but Maya always called her "Momma." She was a strong and loving influence on Maya.

Maya's life took a tragic turn when she was seven. She went to visit her mother in St. Louis. There, her mother's boyfriend sexually abused her. Maya was terrified and ashamed. She only told Bailey what happened. The man was arrested and convicted. Later, he was found dead.

Maya was so shocked by what happened that she stopped speaking. Somehow, she blamed herself for the man's death. She didn't say a word for years. She retreated into silence and refused to communicate.

Maya moved back to the loving care of her grandmother. There, she recalls, she was given "the confidence that I was loved."

During those five years of silence, Maya read constantly. She memorized poems, and even entire books. She read famous African-American poets, like **Paul Lawrence Dunbar** and **Langston Hughes**. She also read Charles Dickens, William Shakespeare, and Edgar Allan Poe. She remembers that she memorized 60 Shakespeare poems and "everything I could find" of Poe. "It was like putting a CD on," she recalled. "If I wanted to, I'd just run through my memory and think, that's one I want to hear."

Eventually, Maya started to speak again. All the reading and memorizing gave her a love of words and language. When she grew up, she learned to speak many languages. She knows Spanish, French, Arabic, and African dialects.

MAYA ANGELOU WENT TO SCHOOL first in Arkansas, then in California. Her mother moved to San Francisco and sent for Maya and Bailey. There, Maya went to Mission High School. She later attended San Francisco Labor School. She studied dance and theater.

FIRST JOBS: Angelou dropped out of school and became a cable car conductor. She was the first black female ever to get the job. By then, she had a son, Guy. Over the next few years she worked several jobs to make a living. She was also briefly married to a man named Tosh Angelos. Later, she would base her last name, Angelou, on Tosh's last name.

In the 1950s, Angelou began a career as a dancer and singer. She sang at famous clubs, like the Purple Onion, in San Francisco. She danced with a young choreographer named **Alvin Ailey**. She toured Europe with a group performing the musical "Porgy and Bess."

STARTING TO WRITE: Angelou moved to New York in the late 1950s. She was singing, writing, and dancing. She performed in plays, wrote poems, and co-wrote a collection of songs performed as *Cabaret for Freedom.* It was a work dedicated to the **CIVIL RIGHTS MOVEMENT** in America.

Angelou believed passionately in the movement for equality for blacks. Dr. Martin Luther King Jr. asked her to lead a section of the Southern Christian Leadership Conference. That's an organization devoted to Civil Rights. She gladly took on the role. (You can read a profile of King in *Biography for Beginners: African-American Leaders, Vol. 1.*) She also fell in love with a leader of the movement for Civil Rights in South Africa, Vusumzi Make.

MOVING TO AFRICA: In 1960, Angelou decided to move to Africa with Make and her son. They lived in Cairo, Egypt. Angelou found work writing for a newspaper, *The Arab Observer.* She later moved to Ghana, where she continued to write for newspapers and magazines. She also taught at the University of Ghana School of Music and Drama.

RETURNING HOME: Angelou returned to the U.S. in 1964. She was hoping to work for leader Malcolm X, whom she'd met in Africa. (See the profile of Malcolm X in *Biography for Beginners: African-American Leaders, Vol. 1.*) Tragically, he was assassinated before they worked together. Angelou continued to work for the Civil Rights movement in the U.S. The assassination of Martin Luther King Jr. in 1968 was a terrible blow to her, and to the entire movement.

A few years later, Angelou began to publish books. Her first major work was *I Know Why the Caged Bird Sings*. It is a memoir of her early life. Despite the despair of those early years, the book is full of hope. It was a great success with adult readers. Soon, Angelou became a well-known author. She published several volumes of poetry that added to her fame. She also wrote both the screenplay and the music for a movie, *Georgia, Georgia.* And she continued to act, too. Over the years, she's appeared in television shows and documentaries. She's a favorite writer of common folk and Presidents, too.

Angelou was chosen by President Gerald Ford to be part of the 200th anniversary of the U.S. in 1976. President Jimmy Carter selected her to be part of the Commission for the International Year of the Woman. And when Bill Clinton was elected President in 1992, he asked Angelou to play a special role as he took the oath of office.

A PRESIDENTIAL INAUGURATION: President Clinton asked Angelou to write a poem for his inauguration. She read the poem, "On the Pulse of Morning," when Clinton was sworn-in as President, in January 1993. It was the first time many Americans had heard her work, and they were impressed.

WRITING FOR CHILDREN: Over her long career, Angelou has also written several books for children. One of the first was *Life Doesn't Frighten Me*. In this book, Angelou writes about things that often scare children: noises, animals, even shadows. The illustrations also vividly reflect those scary images. But, she declares proudly, these things "don't frighten me at all."

Another favorite children's book is *My Painted House, My Friendly Chicken, and Me*. In this book, Angelou tells the story of an African girl, Thandi. Thandi is a member of the Ndebele tribe. Angelou describes her life in her village, including her family and her beloved pet chicken. It is illustrated with beautiful color photographs of tribal life.

In *Kofi and His Magic*, Angelou tells the story of a boy named Kofi. He is from the Ashanti tribe in West Africa. Full of imagination and fun, Kofi invites the reader to visit him and see his village.

Recently, Angelou has written a series of books called *Maya's World*. They describe life in a number of different places, including Italy, Lapland, and France. These countries are seen through the eyes of young people, who bring their homelands to life for young readers.

RECENT WORK: Angelou continues to write and lecture around the world. She's won Grammy awards for her audio recordings of her own work. In December 2005, she was back at the White House. She wrote a special poem "Amazing Peace," for the White House Christmas tree lighting ceremony.

MAYA ANGELOU'S HOME AND FAMILY: Angelou has been married twice. Her first husband was named Tosh Angelos. They were married briefly in the 1950s. In 1973, Angelou married Paul Du Feu. They divorced in 1981. Angelou had a son, Guy, before she married. He's now in his 50's, and he's a writer, too.

Angelou lives in Winston-Salem, North Carolina. She's a professor at Wake Forest University.

HER LEGACY: Angelou is still a vibrant creative artist, still contributing to the world of writing. "I'm happy to be a writer of prose, poetry, every kind of writing. I know of no other art form that we always use. So the writer has to take the most used, most familiar objects—nouns, pronouns, verbs, adverbs—ball them together and make them bounce."

WORLD WIDE WEB SITES:

http://www.achievement.org/
http://www.poets.org/poet.php/prmPID/87
http://www.randomhouse.com/teachers/authors/

Louis Armstrong

1901 - 1971

African-American Trumpeter, Singer, Composer, Actor, and Bandleader

LOUIS ARMSTRONG WAS BORN on August 4, 1901, in New Orleans, Louisiana. His full name was Daniel Louis Armstrong. His parents were Mary Ann and William Armstrong. They were both the descendants of slaves. They were very poor. William left the family soon after Louis's birth. Louis had one sister, Beatrice.

LOUIS ARMSTRONG GREW UP in a poor section of New Orleans. His mother worked hard to support the family. Louis did odd jobs to help out. He worked for a family of peddlers, the Karnoffskys. They sang and played old instruments while they picked up rags and pieces of coal to resell. Louis bought and resold junk and coal in the neighborhood, while blowing on a tiny little trumpet.

When Louis was about seven, he formed a vocal quartet with some friends. They sang on street corners for money. He used the money from singing and odd jobs to buy his first horn. It was a cornet, a smaller version of a trumpet.

LOUIS ARMSTRONG WENT TO SCHOOL only until the fifth grade. When he was 11, he was arrested for shooting off a gun on New Year's Eve. He was sent to reform school.

REFORM SCHOOL: Louis spent 18 months at the Jones Home for Colored Waifs. While he was there, he played in the band. He also got lessons on the horn. After his release, he became a full-time musician. From that point on, his schooling would take place on music stages all over the world.

STARTING TO PLAY: After reform school, Armstrong started playing with the band of trumpeter Joe Oliver, known as King Oliver. Oliver was one of the giants of early jazz. He and others, like Jelly Roll Morton, were taking music in a new direction. They took the rhythms and chord progressions of ragtime music and blues to make something new. It was the birth of jazz.

JAZZ: Jazz music is considered the first American music form. It grew out of several sources. One is African music, brought by enslaved Africans to the U.S. in the 18th and 19th centuries. It also derives from the rhythms and tunes of ragtime, a late-19th century type of music. Ragtime music developed syncopated rhythms—rhythms that experimented with the beat of a piece. Another

Photo of Armstrong from 1946.

source of jazz is the "blues," a style of song noted for repeated phrases.

One of the most important aspects of jazz is "improvisation." In jazz, there is no "set" way to play a piece of music. Instead, players explore the rhythmic and tonal possibilities within a piece's basic framework. So they improvise, or create, tunes around a song's basic structure, like its chords and tonal progressions.

Jazz music developed during the early decades of the 20th century. New Orleans was one of the early "incubators" of jazz. And Louis Armstrong became one its most important, and famous musicians.

King Oliver: King Oliver served as Armstrong's first teacher and father-figure, too. By the early 1920s, Armstrong had absorbed the broad range of music in New Orleans. Every day, he could hear music coming out of clubs, funerals, and parades. There were many great bands playing in New Orleans at the time. King Oliver helped Armstrong get a position in King Ory's band, one of the best.

Armstrong also played on a Mississippi riverboat with the Fate Marable Band. He learned all he could about the new styles coming out of these bands.

In 1922, King Oliver invited Armstrong to join his Creole Jazz Band, then playing in Chicago. So Armstrong moved north. Soon, he was playing second cornet, with Oliver playing first. The jazz experimentation began. Oliver would instruct the band to play only background beats as he and Armstrong played duets and solos. The music was a fantastic hit with audiences. While playing for Oliver, Armstrong met Lil Hardin. She would become his wife and an important influence on him.

FLETCHER HENDERSON: In 1924, Armstrong left the Oliver band to play with Fletcher Henderson. He was one of the great jazz band leaders of the era. Henderson's band included such greats as Coleman Hawkins on sax. Armstrong learned from, and contributed much to Henderson's group.

During this part of his career, Armstrong was also still playing blues. He recorded several outstanding songs with blues greats Bessie Smith and Ma Rainey. Soon, he decided to go back to Chicago. There, he made recording history.

HOT FIVE: Back in Chicago, Armstrong brought together some of the best musicians of the day. Together, they made some of first, and best, jazz recordings in history. Called the Hot Five, the group included Armstrong, his wife Lil Armstrong, Kid Ory, Johnny Dodds, and Johnny St. Cyr.

On songs like "Potato Head Blues" and "Struttin' with Some Barbecue," they introduced the world to the distinctive sound of jazz, as imagined by Louis Armstrong. Under his direction, jazz became a platform for soloists, especially for Armstrong. He played, sang, and spoke his solos, backed up by a tight band.

By this time, Armstrong was playing trumpet instead of cornet. His solos on the instrument truly charted new territory. He expanded its range, with incredible high notes. He punctuated his solos with rhythmic phrasing never heard before.

The recordings of the Hot Five were a sensation. Later, the group became known as the Hot Seven. That group included such greats as Earl Hines on piano. The recordings also featured Armstrong's "scat" singing. Like **Ella Fitzgerald**, Armstrong was a master of scat. In that form, he improvised and sang nonsense syllables to tunes.

In the late 1920s, Armstrong returned to New York City. He played in some of the finest halls. In 1929, he began his acting career, appearing on Broadway in *Hot Chocolate*. The songs were written by the famous Fats Waller. Armstrong made a hit of "Ain't Misbehavin'."

KING OF SWING: The Big Band era of the 1930s and 1940s was named for full orchestras that played popular tunes. It's often called "swing" music, because its tunes and rhythms are great for dancing. The groups often had a major composer, like **Duke Ellington**, as the leader.

Armstrong performing with Ella Fitzgerald, March 30, 1971.

Armstrong started his own Big Band, and they became a world-wide hit. They toured Europe, where audiences loved them. Back home, their recordings topped the charts.

MOVIE STAR: With his music career still hot, Armstrong began to appear in Hollywood movies. He acted in features like *Pennies from Heaven* and *Going Places*. Armstrong even received an Academy Award nomination.

In the late 1940s, Armstrong started a group called The All Stars. They played together for 20 years. Armstrong continued to record, often with other legends of jazz. His series of recordings with **Ella Fitzgerald** are some of the finest of the era. He also recorded with other jazz greats, like Oscar Peterson and Ray Brown, spreading the glory of the music.

MUSICAL AMBASSADOR TO THE WORLD: Armstrong became a beloved figure all over the world. Beginning in the late 1940s, he traveled and performed as part of a goodwill program sponsored by the U.S. State Department. The people of Africa loved him especially.

People everywhere adored the musical ambassador for jazz. He was known for his great playing, but also for his warm personality and great sense of humor. He was known by several affectionate nicknames, including "Satchmo" and "Pops."

Armstrong was popular with people of all ages and backgrounds. He had many hits on Top 40 radio. His version of "Hello Dolly" became one of the biggest hits of the 1960s. In fact, it knocked the Beatles' "I Want to Hold Your Hand" out of the Number One slot in 1964. In 1967, his recording of "What a Wonderful World" became his last pop hit.

LOUIS ARMSTRONG'S HOME AND FAMILY: Armstrong was married four times. His first wife was named Daisy Parker. They were married in 1918. They separated, then divorced when Armstrong moved to Chicago. His second wife was Lil Hardin. They met while playing with the King Oliver band. They were divorced in 1938. Armstrong's third wife was named Alpha Smith. They were married from 1938 to 1942. His fourth wife was Lucille. They were married from 1942 until his death.

Louis Armstrong became ill with pneumonia in 1967, and never regained his health. He died after a heart attack on July 6, 1971. He was mourned throughout the world. More than 25,000 paid their respects at his funeral.

HIS LEGACY: Louis Armstrong is one of the most important figures in the history of jazz. He expanded the form, creating new directions followed by jazz musicians for decades. As a performer, composer, and bandleader, he was one of the most influential musicians of the 20th century.

WORLD WIDE WEB SITES:

http://www.npg.si.edu/exh/armstrong/index.htm
http://www.npr.org/templates/story/story.php?storyId=12208712
http://www.satchmo.net/bio/
http://www.time.com/time/time100/artists/profile/armstrong2.html

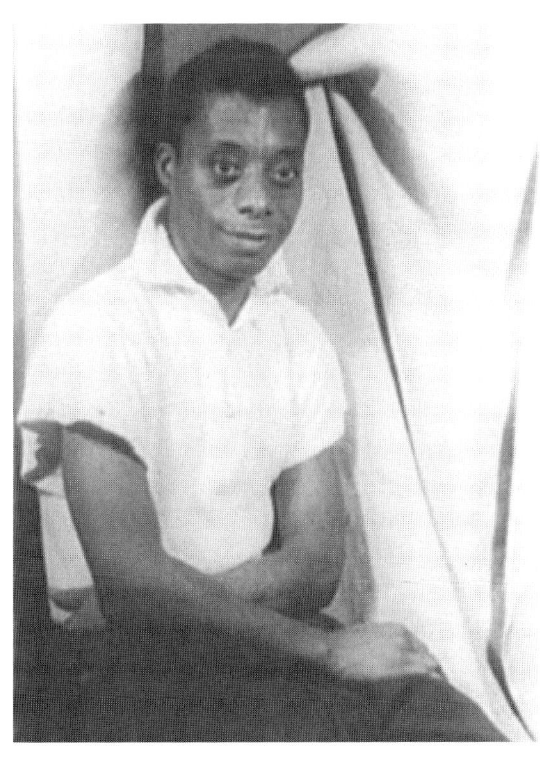

James Baldwin
1924 - 1987
African-American Novelist and Essayist

JAMES BALDWIN WAS BORN on August 2, 1924, in New York City. His mother was named Emma Jones. She was unmarried when James was born. He never knew his birth father. In 1927, Emma married David Baldwin. He became James's stepfather. David Baldwin was a laborer and also a minister.

Emma and David Baldwin had eight children: George, Barbara, Wilmer, David, Gloria, Ruth, Elizabeth, and Paula. James also had a stepbrother, Samuel, from his stepfather's first marriage.

JAMES BALDWIN GREW UP in a poor, unhappy home. "My childhood was awful," he said later. His stepfather was often violent. He also didn't allow his children to take part in the games and pleasures of childhood. James and his siblings couldn't go to movies, listen to music, or even play marbles.

James was afraid of his stepfather, especially his raging temper. Yet as he grew older, he came to understand why his stepfather was so angry. "He had nine children he could barely feed," Baldwin recalled. His stepfather was also the son of a slave. His sense of injustice and his hatred of white people consumed him. "His pain was so great that he translated himself into silence, sometimes into beating us," Baldwin recalled. Finally, his stepfather became mentally ill. He died in a mental hospital.

Baldwin's mother somehow provided love and stability to her children. "My mother was different," he recalled. "She was very gentle." James, as the oldest, helped out with his younger siblings all the time. His mother called him "my right arm. He took care of them all." Baldwin remembered protecting them from "rats, roaches, falling plaster." "I wanted to become rich and famous simply so no one could evict my family again," Baldwin recalled as an adult.

JAMES BALDWIN WENT TO SCHOOL at the local public schools. He went to P.S. 24 and Frederick Douglass Junior High. He was an excellent student, and he loved to read. He spent endless hours at the library. It spurred his desire to be a writer. He claimed that he "began plotting novels at about the time I learned to read."

Baldwin went to De Witt Clinton High School. He was an outstanding student, and he edited the school newspaper and literary magazine.

BECOMING A PREACHER: When he was just 14, Baldwin had a life-changing experience. At a church service, he had a vision of God. He became a preacher, speaking of his experience to others. He preached for several years, but eventually turned his talent to writing.

FIRST JOBS: After high school, Baldwin had to get a paying job to support his family. He worked for a railroad company in New Jersey, and faced brutal racism. It was the time of **JIM CROW**. Although usually associated with the South, Jim Crow laws existed nationwide. They allowed for the legal separation of the races. Blacks were denied equal access to education and public facilities, like theaters and restaurants.

Baldwin recalled his feelings about facing such blatant racism. "I knew about Jim Crow but had never experienced it. I learned in New Jersey that to be a Negro meant, precisely, that one was never looked at but was simply at the mercy of the reflexes the color of one's skin caused in other people."

STARTING TO WRITE: Baldwin was fired from his railroad job. He moved to the Greenwich Village section of New York City. He worked all kinds of odd jobs during the day, and wrote at night. He also received fellowships that provided money to live on, while he wrote.

In the 1940s, Baldwin met **Richard Wright**. Wright was a major author, and he helped Baldwin get his early work published.

LEAVING THE U.S.: When he was 24, Baldwin moved to Paris, France. He felt the outrage of racism in the U.S. deeply. He wanted to be far away from it, and to discover who he was.

GO TELL IT ON THE MOUNTAIN: In 1953, Baldwin published what would be his most famous novel, *Go Tell It on the Mountain*. It was a very personal work. It's about a teenage boy growing up in Harlem. He becomes a preacher and must deal with an angry, jealous father and racism in America. It made him a well-known African-American author.

RETURN TO AMERICA AND THE CIVIL RIGHTS MOVEMENT: Baldwin decided to return to the U.S. in 1956. He'd heard of the growing **CIVIL RIGHTS MOVEMENT**. He wanted to be involved.

Over the next several years, Baldwin traveled in the South. He met Civil Rights leaders like Medgar Evers. He marched for voting rights and against discrimination. He also wrote essays outlining for Americans, black and white, what the problems of the times were. These were collected in well-known works like *The Fire Next Time*.

"I love America more than any country in the world," he wrote. "Exactly for this reason I insist on the right to criticize her perpetually." He continued to write and speak in support of Civil Rights. In the 1960s, the movement sparked violence and assassinations. His friend Medgar Evers was murdered, and Malcolm X and Martin Luther King Jr. were assassinated. (You can read profiles of Evers, Malcolm X, and Martin Luther King Jr. in *Biography for Beginners: African-American Leaders, Vol. 1.*)

Baldwin began to think that peaceful change wasn't possible. He despaired over race relations in America. His writings were full of his disappointment. In 1974, he decided to move back to France.

Baldwin continued to write essays, novels, and plays. He also wrote one children's book, *Little Man, Little Man: A Story of Childhood.* He remained in France until his death.

JAMES BALDWIN'S HOME AND FAMILY: Baldwin never married or had children. He died of cancer on December 1, 1987.

HIS LEGACY: Baldwin wrote passionate works about the racial problems of 20th-century America. In novels, essays, and stories, he tried to make white Americans understand the plight of African-Americans. He influenced other black writers, too. Nobel Prize winner **Toni Morrison** said that Baldwin challenged her "to work and think at the top of my form."

Baldwin claimed he was guided by one purpose. "I want to change the world," he said. "What do I hope to convey? Well, joy, love, the passion to feel how our choices affect the world. That's all."

WORLD WIDE WEB SITES:

http://www.kirjasto.sci.fi/jbaldwin.htm
http://www.pbs.org/wnet/americanmasters/database/baldwin_j.html
http://www.randomhouse.com/features/baldwin/bio.html

Romare Bearden
1911 - 1988
African-American Artist

ROMARE BEARDEN WAS BORN on September 2, 1911, in Charlotte, North Carolina. His parents were Richard Howard and Bessye Bearden. His father was a pianist who worked in the Department of Health in New York City. His mother was a journalist and also founded the Negro Women's Democratic Association. Romare was an only child.

ROMARE BEARDEN GREW UP first in the rural South. He remembered the field hands working in the fields, the women cooking, the trains going by. Even after the family moved North, Romare spent summers in the South with his grandparents.

Romare's parents were both college educated and middle class. They knew that opportunities for African-Americans were limited in the South. It was the time of **JIM CROW**. Legalized segregation limited opportunities for African-Americans, in everything from education to jobs. So they decided to move North.

When Romare was three, the family moved to Harlem, in New York City. It would become an important influence on his life and work. Harlem was the center of African-American art, music, and literature. It was the time of the **HARLEM RENAISSANCE**. His parents knew some of the greatest musicians of the time. Bearden remembered **Duke Ellington** playing piano duets with his dad.

When he was 13, Romare was sent to live with his grandmother in Pittsburgh, Pennsylvania. She ran a boarding house, and Romare enjoyed getting to know the boarders. He also made a new friend, Eugene, who encouraged him to draw. He especially loved to draw cartoons.

ROMARE BEARDEN WENT TO SCHOOL first in New York, then in Pittsburgh. He attended P.S. 139 in Harlem. In Pittsburgh, he attended Peabody High School. He was a good student, and an athlete, too. He played baseball so well that he played pro ball as an adult.

After graduating from high school, Bearden went on to college at Lincoln University. He transferred to Boston University, where he was art director of the student magazine, *Beanpot*. Bearden transferred again, to New York University, where he worked as a cartoonist and art editor for a college magazine. While still in college, he began to draw magazine covers. He graduated with a degree in education.

The Block. *Art © Romane Bearden/Licensed by VAGA, New York, NY*

Bearden continued to study art after college. He attended the Art Students League in New York, and also the Sorbonne, a famous university in France. He kept his hand in cartooning, too. For several years he was the editorial cartoonist for a black newspaper, the *Baltimore Afro-American.*

INFLUENCES: In the 1930s, Bearden met other African-American artists, including **Jacob Lawrence**. He met famous writers like **Langston Hughes** and **Ralph Ellison.** He learned much from them, and shared their devotion to creating a uniquely African-American art.

Bearden joined the Harlem Artists Guild. He studied early European artists, like Giotto, and 20th century masters like Picasso. He learned all he could about the art of all cultures, including African art.

FIRST JOBS: After college, Bearden worked as a social worker with New York City. He worked in that job for 30 years, painting at night. By 1940, he was ready to exhibit his work.

The Block. *Art © Romane Bearden/Licensed by VAGA, New York, NY*

STARTING TO SHOW HIS PAINTINGS: In 1940, Bearden held his first art show in Harlem. When the U.S. entered World War II in 1941, Bearden served his country and put his art career on hold.

During World War II, Bearden served in the Army. He was part of an all-black brigade. After the war, Bearden toured Europe. He studied literature and philosophy, and visited museums, absorbing all he could about art.

Bearden returned to the U.S. In 1944, he had his first national show, in Washington D.C. He was beginning to gain a reputation for his work.

CELEBRATING THE AFRICAN-AMERICAN EXPERIENCE IN ART: From his earliest work, Bearden wanted to celebrate the life of black Americans. He became known for his collage technique.

In works like *The Block,* Bearden used fabric, painting, ink, and photographs to show his vision of street life in Harlem. *The Block* features a series of row houses. Each of the six panels in the work

The Lamp, Art © Romare Bearden/ Licensed by VAGA, New York, NY.

shows a different group of people. There are family scenes and religious scenes. There is joy and sorrow. There are homeless people and people with happy homes. Bearden shows all walks of life, celebrating and sharing in those lives.

Bearden was involved in the **CIVIL RIGHTS MOVEMENT**, too. Along with other artists, he founded a group called Spiral, an organization of African-American artists who worked for equal rights. In 1984, on the 30th anniversary of **BROWN V. THE BOARD OF EDUCATION,** Bearden created a lithograph, *The Lamp*, to commemorate the end of segregation in the schools.

Sometimes Bearden remembered the South of his youth in his art. In works like *Tomorrow I'll be Far Away* he shows a figure full of love for home, but yearning for more. This work is also a collage. Bearden used magazine clippings, wallpaper, spray paint, and charcoal to achieve his vision.

Bearden worked in many different art mediums and styles. He did collage, watercolor, and oil painting. He also created photo montages and prints. Bearden explored other art forms, too. He created costumes and sets for the ballets of **Alvin Ailey**. His wife, Nanette Rohan, was a dancer and choreographer. He created designs for her company, too.

Bearden also did book illustrations, magazine covers, album covers, and sculpture. He even wrote music. One of his songs, "Sea Breeze," became a hit recording for jazz greats Billy Eckstine, Oscar Pettiford, and Dizzy Gillespie. Bearden was an artist of great gifts, which he shared in many different art forms.

Bearden was also devoted to helping young African-American artists. He directed the Harlem Cultural Council. He also helped found The Studio Museum and the Cinque Gallery. Those were places where young artists could show their work and get recognized.

ROMARE BEARDEN'S HOME AND FAMILY: Bearden married Nanette Rohan in 1954. In addition to their home in New York, they had a house on the Caribbean island of St. Martin, where Nanette's parents had been born. Romare Bearden died on March 12, 1988, in New York City. He was 76 years old.

HIS LEGACY: Bearden is considered one of the most important artists of the 20th century. He reflected his love for African-American life in his art. He told the story of everyday life of black Americans in his art, to the rhythms and spirit of jazz music. He was also devoted to helping young artists develop their talents. Today, his works are displayed in some of the country's most important museums.

WORLD WIDE WEB SITES:

http://www.beardenfoundation.org
http://www.metmuseum.org/
http://www.nga.gov/cgi-bin/pbio?246170

Halle Berry
1966 -
African-American Actress
First African-American Woman to Win the Academy Award for Best Actress

HALLE BERRY WAS BORN on August 14, 1966, in Cleveland, Ohio. Her parents are Judith and Jerome Berry. Judith, who is white, is a nurse. Jerome, who is black, worked in a hospital. Halle was the youngest of four children.

HALLE BERRY GREW UP first in the inner city of Cleveland. When she was four, her father left the family and her parents divorced. Her mother moved her children to a mainly white suburb of Cleveland. There, Halle experienced racism for the first time. White children would taunt her because she was biracial. "People would call me zebra and leave Oreo cookies in our mailbox," she recalled.

It was a difficult time for Halle. Her mother sent her to a therapist, to deal with her feelings. She says that it really helped. She learned a "calm and effective way to process emotions." She also decided how she would confront racism. "I became an over-achiever," she said.

HALLE BERRY WENT TO SCHOOL at mostly white public schools. She was an excellent student, and involved in all kinds of activities. She was editor of the newspaper, a member of the honor society, class president, and captain of the cheerleading squad.

When she was in her teens, she won several beauty pageants. She was Miss Teen Ohio and was runner-up in Miss U.S.A. She spent a few terms at Cuyahoga County Community College, studying communications. But she decided she wanted to act instead.

STARTING TO ACT AND MODEL: Berry moved to Chicago and began a career as a model. She also started to take acting classes. Berry moved to New York and began to audition. She landed roles on the TV shows "Living Dolls" and "Knots Landing."

WORKING WITH SPIKE LEE: In 1991, Berry got her first big break. **Spike Lee** cast her in his movie "Jungle Fever." She played a drug addict, and she was convincing and heart breaking in the role.

ALEX HALEY'S "QUEEN": In 1993, Berry won the lead role in "Queen." It was a TV movie based on **Alex Haley's** book, a tribute to his grandmother. Berry shone in the role, and the movie was seen my millions.

Berry wins an Emmy for "Introducing Dorothy Dandridge," Sept. 10, 2000.

Berry's next roles included a film based on the old TV cartoon *The Flintstones.* She also appeared as a former drug addict trying to reclaim her son in *Losing Isaiah.*

***INTRODUCING DOROTHY DANDRIDGE*:** In 1998, Berry decided to take on a new challenge: producer. She wanted to make a movie based on the life of Dorothy Dandridge. Dandridge was an African-American actress with a tragic life marred by racism. Berry both produced and starred in the TV movie, *Introducing Dorothy Dandridge.* She called the work a "turning point in my career." She won several awards for the role, including a Golden Globe and an Emmy.

X-MEN: In 2000, Berry appeared in the first of three *X-Men* movies. They're based on the Marvel comics of the same name. Berry played Storm in the movies, a character who can bring on the power of the weather to fight her foes. Audiences young and old love the movies.

Berry as Storm in X-Men.

AN ACADEMY AWARD: In 2001, Berry appeared in the movie *Monster's Ball.* This movie, for adults, is about a woman whose husband goes to prison. Berry was outstanding in the role, and she won the Academy Award for Best Actress for her performance.

Berry was the first African-American woman ever to win the Oscar for Best Actress. Her acceptance speech was emotional and moving. "This moment is so much bigger than me," she said. "This moment is for Dorothy Dandridge, Lena Horne. And it's for every nameless, faceless woman of color that now has a chance because this door tonight has been opened." Her joy was shared by millions of her fans, who knew how much the award meant.

Berry believes that the power of the award is something she can harness. She wants to help others, in her role as a producer. She's also taken on a wide variety of roles. She's played a superhero, and she's been the voice of a robot in *Robots*. Another important role came in 2005, when she starred in an adaptation of

Their Eyes Were Watching God. It is based on a book by **Zora Neale Hurston,** and was produced by **Oprah Winfrey**.

LIVING WITH DIABETES: Berry has Type 1 diabetes. She makes sure that she eats a healthy diet and gets plenty of exercise. She encourages people of all ages with diabetes to have a healthy lifestyle to control the disease. And she's involved with raising awareness and working with diabetes organizations.

HALLE BERRY'S HOME AND FAMILY: Berry has been married twice. Her first husband was baseball player David Justice. They were married from 1993 to 1997. Her second husband was Eric Benet. They were married from 2001 to 2005. Berry is expecting her first child in 2008, with her boyfriend Gabriel Aubry. She is delighted to become a mother.

HER LEGACY: As the first black woman to win the Academy Award for Best Actress, Berry is an important figure in the history of African-American achievement. She's devoted to opening up the acting world to other women of color to achieve all they can be.

WORLD WIDE WEB SITES:

http://www.biography.com/search/article.do?id=9542339
http://www.imbd.com
http://www.tvguide.com/celebrities/halle-berry/152937

Ray Charles

1930 - 2004

African-American Singer, Songwriter, and Musician
Creator of Such Hit Songs as "Georgia on My Mind," "Hit the Road Jack," and "I Can't Stop Loving You"

RAY CHARLES WAS BORN on September 23, 1930, in Albany, Georgia. His full name was Ray Charles Robinson. His father, Bailey Robinson, was a railroad worker. He left the family when Ray was a baby. Ray and his two siblings were raised by their mother, Aretha Williams. She worked in a sawmill.

RAY CHARLES GREW UP in Greenville, Florida. He had a difficult childhood. His mother worked hard to support the family, but they were very poor. "Even compared to other blacks, we were on the bottom of the ladder looking up at everyone else," Ray remembered. "Nothing below us but the ground."

When Ray was five, his younger brother George died in a tragic accident. The toddler fell into a washtub and drowned. A short time later, Ray developed a serious eye disease called glaucoma. By the time he turned seven, Ray was completely blind. But his mother would not let him feel sorry for himself. She told Ray that he could still lead a normal life. "You might not be able to do things like a person who can see," she said. "But there are always two ways to do everything. You've just got to find the other way."

Music gave Ray a way to escape from his problems. As a boy, he sang in the choir of the local Baptist church. He learned to play piano from a kind shop owner. He also spent many happy hours listening to a wide variety of music on the radio.

RAY CHARLES WENT TO SCHOOL at the St. Augustine School for the Deaf and Blind in Florida. He continued to play piano and learned to play clarinet and saxophone. He also learned to read and write music in Braille (a language of raised letters that blind people read with their fingers).

When Ray was 15 years old, his mother died. The loss made him feel lonely and scared. But he knew that he had to find a way to make it on his own. He decided to leave school and start a career in music. "Music's the only way I've ever thought about making a living," he said.

STARTING A CAREER IN MUSIC: Ray found work playing the piano in a nightclub in Jacksonville, Florida. When he had earned enough money, he moved across the country to Seattle, Washington. In

Charles in a 1964 photo.

these early days, Ray mostly imitated the style of a famous singer, Nat "King" Cole. He played in bars and struggled to support himself.

Luckily, Ray's talent caught the attention of people in the music industry. He got an offer to move to Los Angeles, California, and start a recording career. In 1949 Ray decided to drop his last name so that people would not confuse him with boxer Sugar Ray Robinson. From this time on, he was known as Ray Charles. He recorded songs with several different groups, including the McSon Trio.

In 1952 Charles signed a contract with Atlantic Records and formed his own band. He spent the next few years developing an original sound. His first hit song was "I Got a Woman." It reached the top spot on the rhythm-and-blues (R&B) music charts.

BECOMING THE "FATHER OF SOUL": In 1957 Charles released his first album, *Ray Charles.* The music was unlike anything that had been heard before. Charles combined gospel, blues, jazz, and rock to create a new style. Music critics called it "soul music" and praised Charles as "the father of soul." Lots of other African-American musicians imitated the popular sound.

In 1959 Charles added three female backup singers to his band. The trio became known as the Raelettes. Their sound was very different from Charles's rough, raspy voice. But Charles enjoyed the unusual combination. "I liked that male/female friction and once I had it, I never let it go," he explained.

Charles and the Raelettes released a single, "What'd I Say," that sold over a million copies. It used the call-and-response pattern found in many gospel songs. Some people complained that Charles was being disrespectful to religion. But many others liked his modern update of the gospel sound.

Charles signed a contract with ABC-Paramount Records in 1959. The next year he released a new album, *The Genius of Ray Charles.* It was a huge success. Charles won four Grammy Awards, including best album and best vocal performer of the year. He also won a Grammy for the song "Georgia on My Mind." The Georgia legislature later picked it as the official state song.

CONTINUING TO EXPERIMENT: Charles released several more "Genius" albums that all sold well. But in 1962 he changed his style again. Charles released a new album called *Modern Sounds in Country and Western Music.* Some people criticized him for switching from soul to country. But many others loved his unique, bluesy version of the country sound.

Charles and the Raylettes.

Charles's country album was very popular. One song, "I Can't Stop Loving You," sold two million copies to become the top-selling single of the year. Another song, "Hit the Road, Jack," rose to the number one spot on the pop music charts. Charles liked experimenting with new kinds of music. "I don't want to be branded," he explained. "I don't want the rhythm-and-blues brand, or the pop brand, or any other. That's why I try all these different things."

Just as Charles reached the peak of his career, he got in trouble with the law. In 1964 he was arrested for possession of heroin and marijuana. He admitted that he had been addicted to drugs since age 15. Charles checked himself into a treatment facility in California and quit drugs for good. His successful treatment helped him avoid going to jail. Charles later described his effort to end his drug addiction in a song, "I Don't Need No Doctor."

BECOMING A LEGEND: In the years after he completed his drug treatment, Charles changed his musical style again. He shifted toward a softer, pop sound. Some critics claimed that he stopped experimenting and grew predictable. But Charles's many fans continued to enjoy his music.

In 1973 Charles returned to Atlantic Records. By this time, he was a legend in the music industry. Charles recorded several more albums over the years, and he sold out many concerts. He also performed on television specials and made guest appearances on TV shows. For example, he was a frequent guest on the children's series "Sesame Street." Charles also hosted the comedy show "Saturday Night Live" and appeared in a popular TV commercial for Pepsi-Cola.

Charles was honored with many prestigious awards for his work. In 1983 he won an Image Award from the **National Association for the Advancement of Colored People (NAACP)**. In 1986 he became one of the first artists inducted into the Rock and Roll Hall of Fame. Charles also received a Grammy Award for lifetime achievement in 1987.

FINAL PROJECTS: In 1997 Charles celebrated 50 years in the music business by releasing *Genius and Soul: The 50th Anniversary*

Charles performing on CMT tribute, June 4, 2003.

Collection. Music critics raved about this collection of 101 songs spanning his career. In 2003 Charles recorded an album of duets called *Genius Loves Company.* He sang with some of the biggest names in the recording industry, including B.B. King, Elton John, Bonnie Raitt, Van Morrison, James Taylor, and Diana Krall.

Charles also helped filmmakers create a movie about his life. It was based on a book he published in 1978 called *Brother Ray.* Charles worked with Jamie Foxx, the actor who played him in the film. He also approved the use of his songs in the movie's soundtrack. Unfortunately, Charles did not live to see the finished film. He died of liver disease on June 10, 2004. The music industry mourned the loss of one of its most influential artists.

Both of Charles's final projects became very successful. The movie, *Ray,* won five Academy Awards in 2005. Foxx was honored as best actor for his portrayal of Charles. In addition, *Genius Loves Company* won eight Grammy Awards in 2005, including best album of the year. Charles also received the song of the year award for "Here We Go Again," a duet with Norah Jones.

RAY CHARLES'S HOME AND FAMILY: Charles married Eileen Williams in 1951. They were divorced the following year. In 1955 he married Della Howard. They had three sons together: Ray Charles Robinson, Jr., David Robinson, and Robert Robinson. His second marriage ended in divorce in 1977.

Charles also had love affairs with many different women over the years. He fathered nine more children in these relationships. Before his death, he lived in Los Angeles.

HIS LEGACY: Ray Charles is remembered as one of the finest, most innovative musicians of the 20th century. He was humble about his contribution, always devoted to the music. "Music's been around a long time, and there's going to be music long after Ray Charles is dead. I just want to make my mark, leave something musically good behind. If it's a big record, that's the frosting on the cake, but music's the main meal."

WORLD WIDE WEB SITES:

http://www.raycharles.com

http://www.rockhall.com/inductee/ray-charles

http://www.visionaryproject.com/NVLPmemberTier/visionariesT1/VisionaryPages/CharlesRay

Bill Cosby
1937 -
African-American Comedian, Actor, and Writer

BILL COSBY WAS BORN on July 12, 1937, in Philadelphia, Pennsylvania. His full name is William Henry Cosby Jr. His father, William Cosby Sr. was a sailor in the U.S. Navy. His mother, Anna Pearl Cosby, worked as a maid. Bill had three younger brothers, Russell, Robert, and James. Sadly, James died at a young age.

BILL COSBY GREW UP in the Germantown section of North Philadelphia. His family lived in an all-black, low-income public housing project. His father spent a lot of time at sea on Navy ships.

When Bill Sr. was away, Anna Cosby struggled to raise their boys on her own.

Even as a child, Bill loved comedy. His grandfather often told him long, funny stories. The young boy also enjoyed listening to comedy programs on the radio. "When comedy was on, I was just happy to be alive," he recalled.

BILL COSBY WENT TO SCHOOL in Philadelphia. He attended Wister Elementary School and FitzSimmons Junior High School. Although Bill was very smart, he did not always apply himself to his studies. He often clowned around and told jokes in class. After school, he spent his time playing sports instead of studying.

Bill started out at Central High School, a magnet school for academically gifted students. He competed in sports, appeared in school plays, and worked at several odd jobs. His busy schedule made it hard for him to keep up with his school work. Bill transferred to Germantown High School, but his problems continued. He failed the tenth grade and then dropped out of school.

JOINING THE NAVY: Bill took a job in a shoe repair shop. But he was determined to do something more with his life. In 1956 Cosby joined the U.S. Navy. He received medical training and served in a naval hospital. He did physical therapy on servicemen who had been injured in the Korean War.

During his four years in the Navy, Cosby came to recognize the value of education. He took courses through the mail to earn his high school diploma. In 1961 he won a track and field scholarship to attend Temple University in Philadelphia. He studied physical education and also played fullback on the college's football team.

Cosby left Temple after two years to start his career as a comedian and actor. But he never lost his interest in education. He eventually earned his bachelor's degree from Temple. During the 1970s, he attended graduate school at the University of Massachusetts. He earned a master's degree in 1972 and a doctorate in education in 1977.

BECOMING A STAND-UP COMEDIAN: During his years at Temple, Cosby worked as a bartender at a Philadelphia nightclub. He noticed that he could get bigger tips by making his customers laugh. "I began collecting jokes, and learning how to work them up, stretch them out," he said. Before long, he started performing on stage as a stand-up comedian.

In 1962, Cosby moved to New York City to start a career in comedy. He earned $60 per week for performing at the Gaslight Café. Cosby delighted audiences by telling long, funny stories about his childhood and college years. He often used sound effects, character voices, and silly facial expressions to add to the humor. His act was so popular that the owners of the café soon tripled his salary.

The actor Carl Reiner saw Cosby's show and helped him find a manager. The young comedian's career took off. He performed in top comedy clubs across the country. In 1963 he appeared on national television as a guest on the "Tonight Show." Cosby remembered taking the stage for one of the most important moments of his career. "There was a silence," he noted, "and I said, with a straight face, 'I'd like to talk to you about karate,' and the audience laughed."

Cosby in a scene from "I Spy" with Robert Culp.

In 1964 Cosby released his first comedy album, *Bill Cosby Is a Very Funny Fellow . . . Right!* It was the first of more than 30 popular recordings he would release during his career. Cosby's brand of comedy centered around his life experiences. He found the humor in everyday situations that were shared by many people. Unlike many other African-American comedians, he did not talk about race relations or other controversial issues. Cosby often said that he preferred to focus on the similarities between people, rather than the differences.

BREAKING BARRIERS ON TV: Cosby's successful "Tonight Show" appearance got the attention of television producers. In 1965 he was offered a leading role in a new weekly TV series called "I Spy." Cosby was the first black actor ever to star in a dramatic series on American television.

"I Spy" was an action-adventure show about a pair of undercover secret agents. Cosby and his partner, played by Robert Culp, traveled around the world on spy missions. The show was a big hit with viewers. It remained on the air for three years. Each of these years, Cosby earned an Emmy Award as the most outstanding actor in a dramatic series.

Cosby's role in "I Spy" broke new ground for African-Americans on TV. Still, some TV critics complained because the show did not make his character's race an important issue. Cosby pointed out that "I Spy" was the first series in which a black man and a white man worked together as equal partners. He felt that it presented a positive image of African-Americans.

In 1969 Cosby got a chance to star in his own comedy series, "The Bill Cosby Show." He played Chet Kinkaid, a gym teacher at a Los Angeles high school. During the 1970s, Cosby appeared in several comedy films. One of his most successful films was *Uptown Saturday Night,* released in 1974. Cosby played a taxi driver who tried to recover a winning lottery ticket that was stolen by gangsters. He also became a popular spokesman in TV commercials for such companies as Jell-O, Kodak, Coca-Cola, and Ford.

"THE COSBY SHOW": By the early 1980s, Cosby had grown tired of the types of programs he saw on American television. He was upset by the amount of violence on dramatic series. He also dis-

A scene from the final episode of "The Cosby Show," March 6, 1992.

liked comedy series that featured single parents and sassy, disrespectful children. He decided to create a show that centered around a traditional, middle-class family led by a strong, loving father.

"The Cosby Show" first aired in 1984 and ran until 1992. It was one of the most successful and influential shows of its time. Cosby starred as Cliff Huxtable, a successful doctor and a wise, supportive father. Phylicia Rashad played his wife Clair, a busy lawyer and loving mother. The show focused on the everyday challenges they faced in raising their five children. It was full of gentle, warm-hearted, family humor.

Some critics claimed that "The Cosby Show" was not realistic. They said that the wealthy, educated Huxtable family was too perfect. They argued that the show did not reflect the real-life experiences of most black families in America. But Cosby was proud of the successful series. He felt that it gave viewers of all backgrounds a positive family image that they could identify with.

CREATING TV SHOWS FOR KIDS: As he pursued advanced degrees in education, Cosby became interested in creating educational TV programs for kids. His best-known series is "Fat Albert and the Cosby Kids," which ran from 1972 to 1984. It was a Saturday-morning cartoon about a group of kids growing up in the inner city.

Cosby provided voices for all the characters and also served as host of the show. At the end of each episode, he explained the lesson young viewers could learn from the characters' experiences. Some schools used the "Fat Albert" series as a teaching tool. Cosby wrote a college paper about how the show could be useful to teachers. In 2004 he produced a live-action feature film based on the program.

Beginning in 1998, Cosby served as the host of a TV show called "Kids Say the Darndest Things." The following year, he launched a new cartoon series for preschoolers called "Little Bill." It was based on a popular series of books about Cosby's childhood. It followed the adventures of an imaginative 5-year-old boy and his loving family. TV critics praised the show for teaching young viewers how to solve problems creatively and fairly.

TRAGEDY AND SCANDAL: During the late 1990s and early 2000s, Cosby went through some tough times in his personal life. In January 1997 his son, Ennis, was murdered. Ennis had stopped on the side of a Los Angeles freeway to change a flat tire. Another man robbed and shot him. Cosby founded a charity in his son's memory, the Hello Friend/Ennis William Cosby Foundation. Its mission is to help people identify and treat children with learning disabilities.

Later in 1997, a young woman named Autumn Jackson claimed that Cosby was her biological father. Cosby admitted that he had a brief affair with Jackson's mother in 1973. But he denied that he was the young woman's father. Cosby also said that Jackson had tried to make him pay her $40 million to keep quiet. Jackson eventually went to jail for extortion. (That is using threats or force to try to get money from another person).

In 2006 Cosby was involved in another scandal. A woman accused him of sexually assaulting her in his home. Cosby said that the charges were false. But he decided to pay the woman money to settle her lawsuit. This decision helped him avoid a long, public court trial.

AWARDS: Cosby has become one of the most popular and influential people in the United States. In addition to his achievements as a comedian and actor, Cosby also became a successful author. He shared his wit and wisdom in a number of best-selling books, including *Fatherhood, Love and Marriage,* and *Cosbyology.* In 2003 he published a children's book, *Friends of a Feather: One of Life's Little Fables.* His daughter Erika provided the illustrations.

Cosby has earned many prestigious awards for his creative works. He has won several Grammy Awards for his comedy albums, and several Emmy Awards for his TV roles. In 2002 he received the Presidential Medal of Freedom from President George W. Bush. It is the highest honor the U.S. government can give to a

Cosby marching against violence in Philadelphia, June 4, 2007.

citizen. The award recognized his outstanding contributions to American culture.

SPEAKING HIS MIND: Cosby has tried to use his fame and influence to address problems in American society. He has often criticized the poor quality of TV programs. He has also spoken out about problems in the African-American community.

Cosby first offered his opinion in a famous 2004 speech before the **NATIONAL ASSOCIATION FOR THE ADVANCEMENT OF COLORED PEOPLE (NAACP).** He claimed that black people were too willing to accept high rates of illiteracy, crime, teen pregnancy, and fatherless households. He also criticized the black community's emphasis on sports, fashion, and projecting a tough image. Cosby encouraged black parents to focus on improving their children's education, health, moral values, and self-respect.

Some people criticized Cosby's statements. They said it was not fair for him to blame poor, inner-city blacks for the problems they faced. They claimed that racism kept black communities from getting the resources and opportunities they needed.

In 2007 Cosby published a book about the challenges facing African-Americans. It was called *Come on People: On the Path from Victims to Victors.* He explained that the book's title meant "Let's get moving, let's talk to each other, let's raise the level of our conversation from just saying something to a movement."

BILL COSBY'S HOME AND FAMILY: Cosby met his future wife, Camille Hanks, during his early career as a stand-up comedian. They were married on January 25, 1964. They had one son, Ennis, and four daughters, Erika, Erinn, Ensa, and Evin. Cosby makes his home in Shelburne, Massachusetts.

HIS LEGACY: Cosby is one of the most influential African-Americans in the entertainment field. He is also devoted to helping the African-American community understand and deal with the challenges they face in modern society. In his writings and speeches, he tries to bring his vision for healing the problems of black America to audiences nationwide.

WORLD WIDE WEB SITES:

http://www.billcosby.com
http://www.museum.tv/archives/etv/C/htmlC/cosbybill/cosbybill.htm

Christopher Paul Curtis

1953 -

African-American Writer

Author of *The Watsons Go to Birmingham—1963, Bud, Not Buddy,* and *Elijah of Buxton*

CHRISTOPHER PAUL CURTIS WAS BORN on May 10, 1953, in Flint, Michigan. His parents are Herman and Leslie Curtis. Herman was a hand and foot surgeon who later worked in a car factory. Leslie was a homemaker. Christopher was one of five children. His sisters are Lindsey, Cydney, and Sarah, and his brother is named Herman David.

CHRISTOPHER PAUL CURTIS GREW UP in Flint in a loving but strict family. He was a spirited kid, and he got into mischief.

As some of Curtis's readers have guessed, there's a little bit of his characters in him. Like Byron in *The Watsons*, he used to play with matches. His mom tried to make him stop. She tried to burn his fingertip once, just to let him know how dangerous fire was. But his sister kept blowing out the match. That scene shows up *The Watsons*.

Curtis grew up in a family that loved reading and valued education. "My father would read a book a night," he recalled. Christopher loved to read the family's *World Book* encyclopedia. He looked at the pictures for hours.

CHRISTOPHER PAUL CURTIS WENT TO SCHOOL at Clark Elementary and Southwestern High School in Flint. He did very well in school. His parents wanted him to college after high school, but he went to work in a car factory instead.

WORKING ON THE LINE: Curtis spent 13 years working on the line at a GM plant. He hated it. The money was good, and that's what kept him there so long. But he really wanted to be a writer.

Curtis's job was hanging doors on Buicks. He attached the doors to the cars as they passed by on the assembly line. He was supposed to attach 60 doors per hour. He and a buddy decided to work twice as fast. That way, he'd have time to write.

STARTING TO WRITE: Curtis quit his factory job in 1985. He decided to go to college, at the University of Michigan—Flint campus. He was married with a family, so he worked part-time, too. He kept on writing, and won some prizes for his work.

His wife, Kay, thought he could be an author. She told him to take some time off and work full-time as a writer. She would support the family, in her job as a nurse.

Over the next year, Curtis wrote his first book. He entered the book in two writing contests for young people's fiction. He didn't win, but an editor who'd read his book called him and told him she liked it. Delacorte Press accepted the book, *The Watsons Go to Birmingham—1963*. It was published in 1995.

THE WATSONS GO TO BIRMINGHAM—1963: *The Watsons* takes place in 1963 in Flint. It tells the story of a middle-class black family, the Watsons. The narrator is 10-year-old Kenny Watson.

The book is a funny look at family life that has a serious and touching ending. As the book begins, we learn about the Watsons. Kenny is embarrassed by his family. He calls them the "Weird Watsons." His brother Byron is 13, and becoming a "juvenile delinquent." The parents decide it's time to take Byron South to Grandma, to straighten him out.

The trip to the South is hilarious, full of funny moments. But there is something different about the South. The book takes place in the **JIM CROW** South of the 1960s. At that time, blacks did not have the same rights as whites. In the South, blacks couldn't use the same buildings as white people. They had to use different restaurants, movie theaters, even drinking fountains.

The Watsons visit their grandmother in Birmingham, Alabama. During their visit, a black church is bombed, and four young girls are killed.

The bombing is based on a true incident. In 1963, the 16th Avenue Baptist Church in Birmingham was bombed, and four girls died. In his novel, Curtis shows his readers the power and importance of what happened Birmingham.

The Watsons was a huge success. Curtis was able to quit his job and work full-time as a writer. The book received many awards, including a Newbery Honor. Curtis was delighted with the response. He started work on his next novel.

BUD, NOT BUDDY: Curtis's second novel came out in 1999. It takes place in the Depression of the 1930s. That was a time when many Americans were poor. Many people couldn't find work and were hungry.

Bud, Not Buddy tells the story of 10-year-old Bud Caldwell. He's an orphan living in foster homes and orphanages in Flint, Michigan. He runs away from one horrible foster home and sets out to find the man he thinks is his father.

Along the way, Bud meets other people who are hungry and homeless. He also meets a clever, caring man named Lefty Lewis. Bud also meets a famous jazz musician named Herman E. Calloway. At first, Bud thinks Calloway is his dad. In the end, Bud doesn't find his father, but he does find family and love.

Curtis based two of the characters on his grandfathers. Lefty Lewis is based on his grandfather Earl "Lefty" Lewis. He was a Pullman porter and a pitcher in the Negro Baseball leagues. Herman E. Calloway is based on Curtis's other grandfather, Herman E. Curtis. He was a famous jazz musician.

In *Bud, Not Buddy* Curtis wanted to honor these two men. He says that he ignored the stories he was told about them growing up. He wants his readers to learn from his mistake.

"Be smarter than I was. Go talk to Grandma and Grandpa, Mom and Dad and other relatives and friends. Discover and remember what they have to say about what they learned growing up. By keeping their stories alive you make them, and yourself, immortal."

MORE AWARDS: On January 17, 2000, Curtis learned that he had won two of the most important awards in children's literature. He won the Newbery Award and the Coretta Scott King Award for *Bud, Not Buddy*. He was the first author ever to win both awards. "I'm just overwhelmed," he said.

RECENT BOOKS: Over the past several years, Curtis has continued to produce lively works of fiction for young readers. Favorites include *Bucking the Sarge* and the Mr. Chickee books—*Mr. Chickee's Funny Money* and *Mr. Chickee's Messy Mission.*

***ELIJAH OF BUXTON*:** In 2007, Curtis came out with another award-winning book, *Elijah of Buxton*. It's a story with a very serious theme—the horrors of **SLAVERY**. It takes place in 1860. Elijah is an 11-year-old boy growing up free in Buxton, Canada. That is the site of a settlement of runaway slaves, who fled to freedom in the years leading up to the Civil War. In Canada, Elijah is free, but he returns to the U.S. to right a wrong and witnesses the brutal reality of slavery. The story is fast-paced and fascinating. Readers young and old thrilled to this new story by Curtis. In January 2008, he learned that *Elijah* had won him his second Newbery Honor.

CHRISTOPHER PAUL CURTIS'S HOME AND FAMILY: Curtis met his wife, Kaysandra, when he was working in the factory. Kay is from Jamaica. She grew up in Hamilton, Ontario, in Canada. They have two children, Steven and Cydney.

The family lives in Windsor, Ontario. That's a city in Canada across the river from Detroit, Michigan. Curtis travels all over the country speaking to kids. He talks about his books, and he talks about writing. He really wants to encourage kids, especially African-American kids, to write.

HIS LEGACY: Curtis is devoted to his readers. They inspire him with their questions, and with their own ambitions to be writers. "I always aim my presentation at that one student who might be listening and searching. Maybe I can fan the fire that is already burning inside them. Maybe with a little self-confidence and encouragement, that student will have the nerve to write his or her own *The Watsons Go to Birmingham—1963.*"

WORLD WIDE WEB SITE:

http://falcon.jmu.edu/~ramseyil/curtis.htm
http://www.ala.org/news/2000winners.html
http://www.kidsreads.com/authors/au-curtis-christopher-paul.asp
http://www.randomhouse.com/features/christopherpaulcurtis/

Miles Davis
1926 - 1991
African-American Trumpet Player, Composer, and Bandleader

MILES DAVIS WAS BORN on May 25, 1926, in Alton, Illinois. His full name was Miles Dewey Davis III. His parents were Cleota and Miles Davis Jr. His mother was a musician and his father was an oral surgeon. (That is a doctor who specializes in surgery involving the teeth.)

MILES DAVIS GREW UP in a wealthy family that stressed education and hard work. His mother played the violin and encouraged Miles to study music. His father was an educated black professional who made sure his son understood the racism that limited the opportunities of black Americans.

Miles's father was a follower of Marcus Garvey. Garvey was a Jamaican-born leader who encouraged African-Americans to move to Africa. He thought that America was too racist to allow blacks to achieve equality. Miles Davis Jr. agreed. (You can read a profile of Marcus Garvey in *Biography for Beginners: African-American Leaders, Vol. 1.*)

STUDYING MUSIC: Miles began to study music around the age of ten. While visiting his grandparents in Arkansas, he heard gospel music. That, and the rhythms and tunes he heard on the radio coming out of Harlem were early influences. This was music of the jazz bands of **Louis Armstrong** and **Duke Ellington.**

MILES DAVIS WENT TO SCHOOL at the local public schools in East Saint Louis, Missouri. His family moved there when he was young. Miles's father got him a trumpet when he was 13, which he played in the school band. He did well in school, and loved music especially. When he was still in high school, he got the opportunity to sit in with local bands.

STARTING TO PLAY: Davis played with Eddie Randall's Blue Devils when he was a teenager. They were a swing band, and played music like **Duke Ellington's**. Davis also played in a New Orleans-style band. Their style of swing took a lot from the music of **Louis Armstrong.**

JAZZ: Jazz music is considered the first American music form. It grew out of the rhythms of several sources. One is African music, brought by enslaved Africans to the U.S. in the 18th and 19th centuries. It also derives from the rhythms and tunes of ragtime, a late-19th century type of music. Ragtime music developed syncopated rhythms—rhythms that experimented with the beat of a piece. Another source of jazz is the "blues," a style of song noted for repeated phrases.

One of the most important aspects of jazz is "improvisation." In jazz, there is no "set" way to play a piece of music. Instead, players explore the rhythmic and tonal possibilities within a piece's basic framework. So they improvise, or create, tunes based around the framework of a song—its chord progressions and tonal structure.

INTRODUCTION TO BEBOP: In St. Louis, Davis fell into an incredible opportunity. One night, he'd gone to hear Billy Ekstine's jazz band. It featured two giants of the era, **Dizzy Gillespie** and **Charlie Parker**. (See brief profiles of Gillespie and Parker at the end of the Glossary section.) These two musicians had taken jazz a step further, inventing a form called "bebop."

Unlike the music of the Big Bands, bebop was music to *listen* to, not to dance to. It's full of complex chords and unusual harmonies. Bebop explores the harmonic possibilities, especially in chord progressions, rather than the melodic qualities of a song.

One night, Davis was listening to the band when Gillespie asked him to sit in for the trumpeter, who'd gotten sick. It was a chance to play with two creative geniuses. Davis didn't hesitate. He played with the band for two weeks, learning all he could.

MOVING TO NEW YORK: Davis moved to New York City around 1943. He'd been accepted at the prestigious Julliard School. That's one of the finest music schools in the world. At Julliard, Davis studied classical music, including modern classical composers. These modern composers didn't use conventional scales or rhythms. Davis learned things from them he would use later in improvising jazz music.

Davis dropped out of Julliard after a while. He decided he wanted to play with other jazz musicians. Over the next few years, he played with Charlie Parker's group. He toured New York and California, where a new style of jazz was developing.

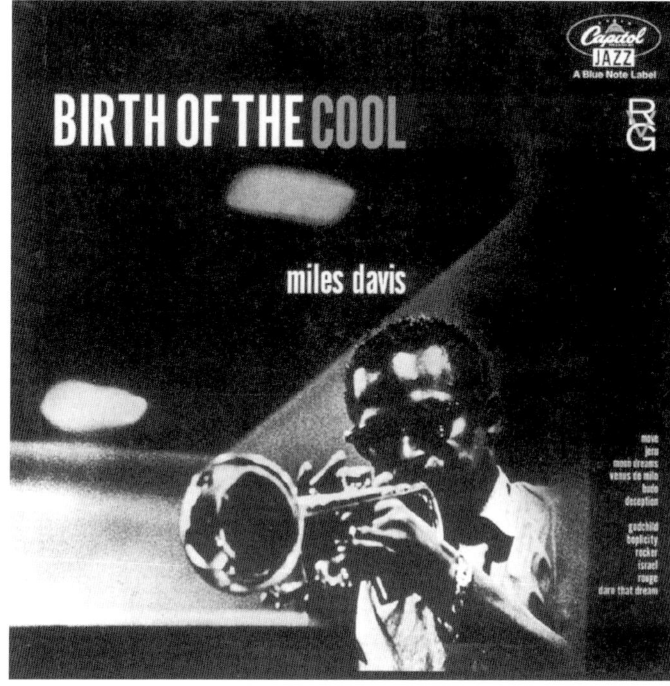

BIRTH OF THE COOL: The kind of music Davis was playing became known as "cool" jazz. It was different from the "hot" jazz of the era. It was slower and quieter. Its rhythms were less intense. Together with great musicians like Gerry Mulligan on sax and Gil Evans on piano, Davis made some very important recordings. They were released as *Birth of the Cool* in 1950.

HIS STYLE: Davis always had a distinctive style on trumpet. He liked to "bend" notes, over and under the pitch. He often played with his Harmon mute in place, which made for a quieter sound. He liked to play simple, melodic lines, not the faster, more frantic runs of bebop players like Gillespie.

DRUG ADDICTION: Tragically, this gifted musician also suffered with drug addiction. He began to take drugs in the 1940s, and struggled with addiction for years. In 1954, he was able to quit and started one of the most creative periods of his life.

***MILES DAVIS AND THE MODERN JAZZ GIANTS*:** Davis made many landmark recordings in his career. One was *Miles Davis and the Modern Jazz Giants.* As the title indicates, it includes some of the greatest jazz players of the era. The record, from 1954, includes Davis, Milt Jackson, Thelonious Monk, Percy Heath, and Kenny Clark. Tracks like "The Man I Love" showcase the ensemble's close understanding of the tonal possibilities of the piece. And it also reveals the almost telepathic way the musicians could communicate while making music.

MILES DAVIS QUINTET: Davis formed a quintet in the mid-1950s featuring other jazz greats. The group included John Coltrane, Red Garland, Paul Chambers, Philly Joe Jones, and Davis. They produced songs like "'Round Midnight" that became standards of the modern jazz era.

KIND OF BLUE: In 1959, Davis released *Kind of Blue*. It has been called the most important jazz recording ever made. The musicians were some of the best ever. Cannonball Adderly, John Coltrane, Wyn Kelly, Bill Evans, Paul Chambers, and James Cobb joined Davis to produce songs like "So What." These recordings feature a tight ensemble devoted to group improvisation. Piano player Bill Evans noted that what they produced was "something close to pure spontaneity." Davis's other important recordings of the era include *Porgy and Bess* and *Sketches of Spain.*

JAZZ FUSION: In the 1960s, Davis took his music in a new direction. He combined jazz with rock in a sound called "jazz fusion." It featured electronic instruments and the influence of rock musicians like Jimi Hendrix. Some of Davis's fans loved it. Many didn't. But Davis was a musician who needed to explore and change. His bands of the 1960s and 1970s included young musicians like Chick Corea and Keith Jarrett.

Davis performing in Tel Aviv, Israel, June 1, 1987.

LATER YEARS: In the 1970s, Davis had many health problems. He continued to battle drug addiction, and he was in a serious car accident. He made more recordings in the 1980s, and toured again. One of his last recordings, *Decoy*, won a Grammy award. His health began to fail, however. He died on September 28, 1991, following a stroke and respiratory illness.

MILES DAVIS'S HOME AND FAMILY: Davis was married four times. He married his first wife around 1943. They had one son and later divorced. He married Frances Taylor in 1958; they divorced in 1968. In 1968, he married Betty Mayby; they divorced one year later. His fourth wife was actress Cicely Tyson. They were married from 1981 to 1988.

HIS LEGACY: Miles Davis is considered one of the most important jazz musicians in history. He took jazz music into a more complex, serious era, incorporating ideas from many different sources and leaving his own unique signature on major jazz works.

WORLD WIDE WEB SITES:

http://www.legacyrecordings.com/Miles-Davis.aspx
http://www.milesdavis.com/
http://www.pbs.org/jazz/biography/artist_id_davis_miles.htm
http://www.rockhall.com/inductee/miles-davis

Ossie Davis
1917 - 2005
African-American Actor, Writer, Activist, Director, and Producer

OSSIE DAVIS WAS BORN on December 18, 1917, in Cogdell, Georgia. His name when he was born was Raiford Chatman Davis. He got the name "Ossie" when the clerk registering his name misheard his mother. She had given his initials, "R.C." The clerk thought she said "Ossie." The name stuck.

Ossie's parents were Laura and Kince Davis. Laura was a homemaker and Kince was a railroad construction worker. Ossie was the oldest of five children.

Ossie grew up in a family of storytellers. That, and his love for his parents, inspired him to want to become a writer. "Daddy was in my life, a mythical hero," he recalled. "As was my mother. I decided to become a writer so that I could tell their stories."

His father couldn't read, but that didn't hurt his storytelling abilities. "He took life and broke it up in little pieces and fed it to us like little birds," Davis remembered. And, he recalls, there weren't the other distractions of modern life. "We didn't have the disadvantages of television in those days. My imagination caught fire and I have never been able to put the fire out."

OSSIE DAVIS WENT TO SCHOOL at the local public schools. He did well in school, and won a scholarship to the Tuskegee Institute. But the scholarship only covered classes. It didn't include money for room and board. It looked like Davis wouldn't get to college. But then he got a scholarship to Howard University in Washington, D.C. Howard is one of the finest traditional black colleges in the country. And because Davis had aunts living in Washington, he lived with them while going to school.

Davis loved college. While he was a student he was able to hear **Marian Anderson's** famous performance on the steps of the Lincoln Memorial. It made a great impact on him. "I understood fully, for the first time, the importance of black song, black music, black arts," he said. "I was handed my spiritual assignment."

Davis studied with the famous black scholar Alain Locke. Locke encouraged him to explore the arts, and to write plays. He also encouraged Davis to go New York and study acting. Davis graduated from Howard in 1939. He moved to New York, ready to start a new life.

Davis as Gabriel in The Green Pastures, *1951.*

STARTING TO PERFORM: In New York, Davis performed with the Rose McClendon Players. He first appeared on the stage in 1939.

WORLD WAR II: When the U.S. entered World War II in 1941, Davis served in the Army. He worked for several years with an all African-American surgical team. He spent most of the war in Libya. There, he helped wounded soldiers recover and return to the U.S.

ACTIVISM: After the war, Davis got involved in social activism. "When World War II was over, there was a strong feeling in the country that racism had to be attacked," he recalled. "The artistic community seemed to be leading the way." So when he returned to the U.S. in 1945, he started working for social change. In the 1950s, when anti-Communist feeling threatened individual liberties, he spoke out, bravely, against it.

ACTING: Back in New York in 1946, Davis won the lead in play called *Jeb.* Starring with him was a young actress named **Ruby Dee.** They became friends, then fell in love and married. They created a lifelong partnership devoted to their craft and their family.

In 1950, Davis and Dee made their film debuts together. They appeared, with **Sidney Poitier**, in a movie called *No Way Out*, about

Davis as Da Mayor, with Spike Lee as Mookie, in Do the Right Thing, *1989.*

racism. In 1955, Davis appeared in a television version of Eugene O'Neill's powerful *Emperor Jones.* In 1959, Davis appeared in **Lorraine Hansbery's** groundbreaking play, *A Raisin in the Sun.*

Despite their talent and their success, Davis and Dee often had trouble landing good roles. But that didn't stop them. They performed in churches and schools, reaching out to the community and sharing their love of theater.

CIVIL RIGHTS MOVEMENT: Davis and Dee believed deeply in the struggle for equality and civil rights. They became involved in the movement in many ways. They took part in the March on Washington in 1963. They spoke and wrote about equal rights.

Their close friends included Martin Luther King Jr., W.E.B. Du Bois, and Malcolm X. (You can read profiles of King, Du Bois, and Malcolm X in *Biography for Beginners: African-American Leaders, Vol. 1.*) After Malcolm X's assassination in 1965, Ossie Davis gave the eulogy at his funeral. His belief in the goals of the Civil Rights Movement gave essence to the roles he chose, and the direction of his career.

WRITING AND DIRECTING: Davis continued to write plays, and in 1961, he had success with *Purlie Victorious*. The play tells the story of a black preacher named Purlie who tries to integrate his church. Dee starred in the play, which was later made into a movie, *Gone Are the Days*. Davis rewrote the play as a musical, *Purlie*, which became a Broadway hit.

Davis also appeared in many TV shows over the years. He acted in episodes of well-known shows, like *The Fugitive* and *Bonanza.* And he developed a reputation as a writer and director for his movie, *Cotton Comes to Harlem.* The film featured two Harlem police detectives, trying to solve a crime. It was a great hit for Davis.

THE MOVIES OF SPIKE LEE: Over the years, Davis and Dee also appeared in many of **Spike Lee's** movies. In *Jungle Fever*, Davis plays the father of a child lost to drug addiction. In *Do the Right Thing* he plays Da Mayor, in love with Mother Sister (played by Dee). In *Malcolm X*, Davis delivers the eulogy for Malcolm he gave in real life, this time set down on film for posterity.

MORE PRODUCTIONS WITH RUBY DEE: Davis and Dee also created several successful shows for television. In 1980, they created *With Ossie and Ruby.* They later published an autobiography with the same name. In 1986, the produced a TV special titled *Martin*

Luther King: The Dream and the Drum. They co-produced another special on the theme of Civil Rights, *Promised Land*, in 1996. The two appeared in *Roots: The Next Generation*, a continuation of **Alex Haley's** saga.

LATER YEARS: Davis continued to work into his late 80s. In 1992, he published a novel for young adults, *Just Like Martin*. Davis was working on a new movie, *Retirement*, when he died on February 4, 2005. He was 87 years old. People everywhere mourned the passing of this great actor and humanitarian. Thousands attended his funeral in New York.

Ossie Davis and Ruby Dee, 2004.

OSSIE DAVIS'S HOME AND FAMILY: Davis was married for 57 years to actress and activist **Ruby Dee.** They had three children, Nora, Guy, and LaVerne. The couple had a very close and loving marriage. They shared their commitment to family, acting, and Civil Rights in all their years together. "We had a common understanding," Davis said. "We believe in honesty. We believe in simplicity. We believe in love. We believe in family. We believe in Black history. And we believe heavily in involvement."

HIS LEGACY: Ossie Davis is a giant in the world of acting and activism. He was also devoted to improving the opportunities of African-Americans in every walk of life. He and Dee were honored with a lifetime achievement award by the Kennedy Center in 2004. They were noted for "opening many a door previously shut tight to African-American artists and planting a seed for the flowering of America's multicultural humanity."

WORLD WIDE WEB SITES:

http://newsinfo.iu.edu/news/page/normal/200.html
http://www.kennedy-center.org/calendar/index.cfm?fuseaction=showIn
http://www.npr.org/templates/story/story.php?storyId=1119605
http://www.pbs.org/wnet/aaworld/reference/articles/ossie_davis.html

Ruby Dee

1924 -

African-American Actress, Writer, and Activist

RUBY DEE WAS BORN on October 27, 1924, in Cleveland, Ohio. Her name when she was born was Ruby Ann Wallace. She later took the name "Ruby Dee" as her "stage," or performing name.

Her parents were Marshall and Emma Wallace. Marshall worked for the railroad as a porter. Emma was a teacher. They moved their family from Cleveland to New York when Ruby was little. They wanted to provide more opportunities to their children.

RUBY DEE GREW UP in a loving middle-class family. They lived in the Harlem section of New York. Her parents expected a lot from her, and she worked hard to meet those expectations. Emma Wallace wanted her children to know about literature and art. She read poetry to them, including the work of African-American **Paul Laurence Dunbar.**

RUBY DEE WENT TO SCHOOL at a private school in New York City. She wanted to be challenged academically. So she went to the mostly-white Hunter High School. She was an outstanding student. She also wrote poetry, which she sent to local newspapers.

Ruby began to appear in school plays, and knew that she loved to act. She recalled that "one beautiful afternoon I read aloud from a play and my classmates applauded." She'd found what she wanted to do for the rest of her life.

After high school, Ruby went on to Hunter College in New York. She joined the American Negro Theater. It was the home of several up-and-coming African-American actors. She met **Sidney Poitier** and Harry Belafonte**.** They worked for little or no money, doing everything from casting and acting to cleaning up. It was wonderful training.

It was at this time that she took the stage name "Ruby Dee." It was the name she's made famous over a career of more than 60 years.

EARLY ACTING ROLES: In 1946, Dee landed a role in a play called *Jeb.* It was about an African-American soldier returning from World War II. The lead in the play was a young actor named **Ossie Davis**. They became friends, fell in love, and married on December 9, 1948. It was the beginning of an important, lifelong partnership.

After *Jeb,* Dee and Davis appeared in *Anna Lucasta* and *Smile of the World.* They performed in New York and all over the country in a traveling company. They appeared in an important film about racism, *No Way Out*, with **Sidney Poitier.** While they often performed together, Dee also established her own career, playing roles for the stage, film, and television.

THE JACKIE ROBINSON STORY: One of Dee's important early roles came in 1950. She played the wife of baseball player Jackie Robinson, who broke the color line in baseball in 1946. (You can read a profile of Robinson in *Biography for Beginners: African-American Leaders, Vol. 1.*)

Dee made several movies during the late 1940s and 1950s. She also continued to appear on the stage. In Ossie Davis's *Purlie Victorious*, she starred in one of her finest roles. As Lutiebelle Gussie Mae Jenkins, she played a spirited woman opposite Davis as Purlie. The play was made into the very successful musical, *Purlie*.

A RAISIN IN THE SUN: On March 1, 1959, Dee debuted in one of the most important roles of her career. She played the wife of **Sidney Poitier** in **Lorraine Hansberry's** *A Raisin in the Sun* on Broadway. It was a tremendous hit, which surprised everybody, including Hansberry. It was the first play on Broadway with an all-black cast and director. It was also the first to portray African-American life. Dee and Poitier went on to star in the successful film version of the play in 1963.

GETTING INVOLVED IN THE CIVIL RIGHTS MOVEMENT: Dee and Davis were both actively involved in the **CIVIL RIGHTS MOVEMENT**. They were members of the **NAACP** and took part in several

Ruby Dee in The Jackie Robinson Story, *with Richard Lane, Jackie Robinson, and Billy Wayne, 1950.*

demonstrations during the 1960s. They also wrote, directed, and produced several films about the movement over the years. They were also fierce defenders of civil rights in the 1950s, when anti-Communist fury threatened individual freedoms.

STAGE ROLES: Dee continued to act in stage productions, in addition to working in films and television. In 1970, she appeared in *Boesman and Lena*. The play is by Nobel-prize winning dramatist Athol Fugard. He is a white South African, and the play takes place in South Africa. Dee played Lena, married to Boesman, who was played by **James Earl Jones.** The play explores the problems of

Dee, as Mother Sister, and Davis, as Da Mayor, in Do the Right Thing, *1989.*

race, especially of mixed race people. Dee loved the role. She said that in the character of Lena she was as "alive as I've never been on stage."

Dee became the first African-American actress to play major parts in The American Shakespeare Festival. She played leading roles in *The Taming of the Shrew* and *King Lear* in 1965.

Dee has always performed a wide variety of plays. She's appeared in the work of French playwright Jean Genet. She won an award for her performance in American Eugene O'Neill's *Long Day's Journey into Night.* In 1998, Dee appeared on stage in a one-woman show based on her memoir, *One Good Nerve.*

TELEVISION ROLES: Dee played many roles on television, too. She appeared in long-running shows like *The Defenders* and *Peyton*

Place. She won an Emmy for her performance in *Decoration Day*. In 1979, Dee and Davis appeared in *Roots: The Next Generation*. It was the sequel to **Alex Haley's** legendary *Roots*. Dee played Haley's grandmother.

Dee as Mother Sister, in Do the Right Thing, *1989.*

Dee and Davis also created several successful shows for television. In 1986, they produced a TV special titled *Martin Luther King: The Dream and the Drum*. (You can read a profile of Martin Luther King Jr. in *Biography for Beginners: African-American Leaders, Vol. 1.*) They co-produced another special on the theme of Civil Rights, *Promised Land*, in 1996.

THE FILMS OF SPIKE LEE: Dee and Davis appeared together in several of the films of **Spike Lee**. One of their most moving performances was in *Do the Right Thing*. Dee plays Mother Sister, who observes the neighborhood from her apartment window. Davis plays Da Mayor, who sweetly courts Mother Sister.

MANY HONORS AND AWARDS: Dee has received many honors and awards. She (and Davis) received a lifetime achievement award from the Kennedy Center. They also received a lifetime achievement award from the Screen Actors Guild. Her final audio album with Davis won a Grammy.

Ossie Davis died on February 4, 2005. He was mourned by millions. His death marked the end of one of the most celebrated collaborations in American history.

Ruby Dee continues to appear in television and films. In 2005, she appeared in a TV adaptation of *Their Eyes Were Watching God.* It is based on a book by **Zora Neale Hurston,** and was produced by **Oprah Winfrey**. In the fall of 2007, she appeared with **Denzel Washington** in *American Gangster.* In January 2008, Ruby Dee received a Screen Actors Guild Award and an Academy Award nomination for her role in that film.

RUBY DEE'S HOME AND FAMILY: Ruby Dee and Ossie Davis married in 1948 and were together for 57 years. They had three children, Nora, Guy, and LaVerne. Their marriage was legendary. They shared a commitment to family, to the struggle for Civil Rights, and most of all, to each other.

HER LEGACY: Ruby Dee's legacy is one of commitment to her craft and to social justice. When she and her husband received an award from the Screen Actors Guild, they were praised for their contributions to American culture. "For more than half a century, they have enriched and transformed American life as brilliant actors, writers, directors, producers, and passionate advocates for social justice, human dignity, and creative excellence."

WORLD WIDE WEB SITES:

http://newsinfo.iu.edu/news/page/normal/200.html
http://www.kennedy-center.org/calendar/index.cfm?fuseaction=howIn
http://www.npr.org/templates/story/story.php?storyId=1119605
http://www.pbs.org/wnet/aaworld/reference/articles/ruby_dee.html

Paul Laurence Dunbar
1872 - 1906
African-American Poet, Essayist, Novelist, and Short Story Writer

PAUL LAURENCE DUNBAR WAS BORN on June 27, 1872, in Dayton, Ohio. His parents were Matilda and Joshua Dunbar. Matilda had been a slave in Kentucky until the Civil War. Joshua had escaped slavery and served in the Union Army during the war. They separated soon after Paul's birth. After Joshua left, Matilda made her living washing clothes. Paul had two half-siblings from his mother's second marriage.

PAUL LAURENCE DUNBAR GREW UP with his family in Dayton. His mother always encouraged her children to do well in school and to read. She entertained them with stories and songs. Paul began to read very early, and by the age of six was writing poems.

PAUL LAURENCE DUNBAR WENT TO SCHOOL at the local public schools. One of his classmates and friends was Wilbur Wright. Dunbar attended Central High School, where he was the only African-American.

Dunbar did well in school, and also edited the school paper, where he published his first poems. He also edited the school's literary magazine and competed on the debate team. When he was 17, he started a newspaper, *The Dayton Tattler*, printed by the Wright Brothers.

FIRST JOBS: Even though he was an excellent student, Dunbar couldn't afford college. After graduating from high school, he got a job as an elevator operator. He spent all his free time writing poems.

In 1892, a former teacher asked him to read his poems at the Western Association of Writers conference. The gathered writers listened eagerly to his work. One wrote a letter to a local newspaper praising Dunbar's poetry. The letter circulated, and soon many more people were interested in Dunbar.

FIRST POETRY COLLECTION: Dunbar decided to publish a collection of his poetry on his own. It was titled *Oak and Ivy*, and was published in 1893, for $125. It didn't make much money, and Dunbar kept working as an elevator operator. He sold as many copies of his book as he could, often to people riding his elevator, for $1.

In 1893, Dunbar moved briefly to Chicago. It was the time of the World Columbian Exhibition. He met Frederick Douglass, the great **ABOLITIONIST** and orator. (You can read a profile of Frederick Douglass in *Biography for Beginners: African-American Leaders, Volume 1.*)

Douglass got Dunbar a job as a clerk at the Exhibition. He arranged for Dunbar to give a poetry reading. He also championed his work. He called Dunbar "the most promising young colored man in America."

Dunbar returned from Chicago to his job as an elevator operator. He sent his poems to magazines and newspapers, and finally, they were published. Around this time, he met the head of a Toledo mental hospital, Dr. Henry Tobey. Tobey paid for the printing of Dunbar's second poetry collection. It was called *Majors and Minors* and appeared in 1895.

Majors and Minors is Dunbar's best-known collection. It contained the two types of poems for which he became famous. One, the "Majors," were original poems on many subjects in standard English. The "Minor" poems were written in African-American dialect. Many of them are set in African-American communities. Some are retellings of the folktales and songs his mother told him when he was little. These poems were widely praised at the time.

The collection received a wonderful review in *Harper's Weekly.* That was one of the most important magazines of the time. The review was written by William Dean Howells, the era's most important critic.

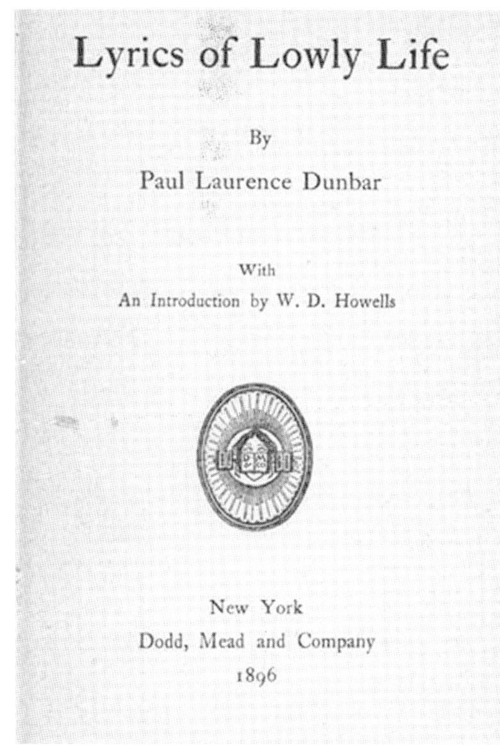

Lyrics of Lowly Life

By

Paul Laurence Dunbar

With

An Introduction by W. D. Howells

New York

Dodd, Mead and Company

1896

A FAMOUS POET: Dunbar became a well-known poet. He traveled around the country. A New York publisher printed his next book, *Lyrics of a Lowly Life*. It included all the poems from Dunbar's first two books, with an introduction by Howells.

Dunbar traveled to England to read his poetry and promote his books. When he returned, he got a job at the Library of Congress. He continued to write poems, and also stories, a novel, and song lyrics. He left the Library in 1898 to write full-time.

Dunbar wrote many poems that focused on the unfair treatment of African- Americans. In "We Wear the Mask," he says, "We wear the mask that grins and lies," describing how blacks must act around whites. Yet it was his poems written in dialect that were his most famous. Some feature life on the plantation, and are written in the language of poor, uneducated blacks. Some modern readers have a difficult time with them. The subject matter and the dialect are, for some, demeaning. But for many readers, they do not detract from his overall contribution.

Dunbar became a celebrated writer. He published 12 books of poetry, a play, several novels, and four short stories collections in his brief life. His work is still widely read and admired.

PAUL LAURENCE DUNBAR'S HOME AND FAMILY: Dunbar married Alice Ruth Moore, a fellow poet, in 1898. They separated in 1902. Dunbar became very depressed and began to drink heavily. He was also ill with tuberculosis (TB). TB is a disease that destroys the lungs. When Dunbar became sick, there was no cure. He moved back to his mother's house in Dayton, Ohio. He died of TB on February 9, 1906. He was 33 years old.

HIS LEGACY: Dunbar is considered the first important African-American poet. His works were widely read in his time, and still studied by students today. His poems capture the African-American experience of his era. They celebrate the folklore and culture of a time that has disappeared. They also speak for generations of African-Americans proudly struggling for equality.

WORLD WIDE WEB SITES:

http://www.dunbarsite.org
http://www.libraries.wright.edu/special/dunbar
http://www.poets.org/pot.php/prmPID/302

Duke Ellington

1899 - 1974

African-American Composer, Bandleader, and Piano Player

DUKE ELLINGTON WAS BORN on April 29, 1899, in Washington, D.C. His name when he was born was Edward Kennedy Ellington. He got the nickname "Duke" for his love of fancy clothes and stylish ways.

His parents were James and Daisy Ellington. James worked as a butler, sometimes filling in at the White House. Daisy was a homemaker who came from a respected Washington family.

DUKE ELLINGTON GREW UP in a loving, solidly middle class family. His home was full of books, culture, and conversation. His parents were very religious, and they loved music. They both played the piano, and Duke started lessons at age seven. But he didn't like lessons that much. He was more interested in art. And he loved baseball. Duke's first job was selling peanuts at Washington Senators' baseball games.

DUKE ELLINGTON WENT TO SCHOOL at the local public schools. He attended Armstrong High School, where he studied art. He won a college scholarship to Pratt Institute in New York. But by his senior year in high school, Ellington was sure he wanted a career in music. He dropped out of school at 17. He made his living painting signs by day and playing music at night.

EARLY MUSIC: Ellington formed his first band, The Washingtonians, when he was a teenager. He started composing when he was 15 years old. Amazingly, he never learned to read music. Instead, his son Mercer said, he was "self-taught, learning by ear." "It was the hard way of doing it," Mercer recalled. "But it was the way he preferred, even if it took more time and cost him more energy."

Ellington's early work was influenced by the piano style known as "ragtime." Ragtime music featured syncopated rhythms—rhythms that experimented with the beat of a piece. Soon, Ellington began to compose for the individual members of his band. It was a method he would use throughout his creative life, to showcase the individual gifts of his enormously talented bandsmen.

MOVING TO NEW YORK: In the 1920s, Elllington and his band moved to New York City, the center for early jazz. It was also the

Ellington around age five.

time of the **HARLEM RENAISSANCE.** African-Americans from all over the country congregated in Harlem to write, paint, and make music. Their works celebrated the African-American experience. It was a time of great hope, and artistic richness.

In New York, Ellington and his band played at the Kentucky Club. Next, they got work at the legendary Cotton Club.

THE COTTON CLUB: Harlem's Cotton Club was world-famous for its African-American performers. It was the premier showcase for black singers, dancers, and bands in the country. Duke Ellington and his Famous Orchestra played as regulars at the Cotton Club for three years. That included weekly radio broadcasts, which made them famous nationwide. Ellington songs from this era include "Black and Tan Fantasy" and "The Mooche." They were some of the earliest formal jazz compositions.

JAZZ: Jazz music is considered the first American music form. It grew out of several sources. One is African music, brought by enslaved Africans to the U.S. in the 18th and 19th centuries. It also derives from the rhythms and tunes of ragtime. Another source of jazz is the "blues," a style of song noted for repeated phrases.

One of the most important aspects of jazz is "improvisation." In jazz, there is no "set" way to play a piece of music. Instead, players explore the rhythmic and tonal possibilities within a piece's basic framework. So they improvise, or create, tunes based around the framework of a song—its chord progressions and tonal qualities.

SHOWCASING THE TALENT OF HIS ORCHESTRA: Ellington wrote most of the music played by his orchestra. His talent as a composer drew some of the finest jazz players in the land. They included world-famous players like Cootie Williams on trumpet, Ben Webster on sax, Juan Tizol on trombone, and Barney Bigard on clarinet.

Many of these gifted musicians played with Ellington for years. Over those years, he wrote pieces that revealed their amazing talents. His compositions displayed their musical gifts and strengths, featuring intricate harmonies, muted brass, and striking combinations of instruments.

THE BIG BAND ERA: Ellington's orchestra became known as one of the greatest of the Big Bands. The Big Band era of the 1930s and 1940s was named for full orchestras that played popular tunes. It's often called "swing" music, because its tunes and rhythms are great for dancing. The groups often had a major composer, like Ellington, as the leader.

WRITING FOR THE STAGE AND MOVIES: Ellington's creative talent spread beyond the band stage. He composed music for Broadway, including *Chocolate Kiddies.* He wrote music for movies, too, including *Check and Double Check.*

FACING DISCRIMINATION: Even though they were one of the most successful bands of the era, Ellington's orchestra faced racial prejudice. At the Cotton Club, African-Americans were the featured

Ellington directing his band from the piano, New York, 1943.

talent, but weren't allowed in as customers. When the band traveled in the South, they faced **JIM CROW** segregation. They couldn't find places to eat or sleep. In 1930, when they appeared in the movie *Check and Double Check*, trombone player Juan Tizol had to put on black makeup—blackface. The movie makers didn't want people to know that the band was integrated.

All the discrimination he faced just fueled Ellington's creativity. He wrote some of his greatest music, like *Black, Brown, and Beige*, as tributes to African-Americans and their struggle for equality. "I took the energy it takes to pout and wrote some blues," he said.

BILLY STRAYHORN: In 1939, Billy Strayhorn joined the Ellington band. He was a remarkable composer. He and Ellington wrote some of the best music the group ever performed, including their signature piece, "Take the 'A' Train." Ellington and Strayhorn collaborated on some of the greatest songs of the 20th century. Among them are the soulful "Sophisticated Lady" and "Chelsea Bridge." The two also wrote movie music, including the score to *Anatomy of a Murder.*

TRAVELING THE WORLD: Ellington and his band traveled around the world. It's estimated that they played 20,000 performances

*Ellington in his dressing room,
with his piano and wardrobe, 1946.*

worldwide, traveling 10 million miles to 65 countries. They found admiring audiences everywhere. They performed in the Middle East, India, Pakistan, Iran, Iraq, and Lebanon. Ellington often gave talks at these concerts, introducing his audiences to the history of jazz.

During the 1940s, Ellington began a series of concerts at Carnegie Hall. They showcased a major new work each year. This was the place he premiered works like *Black, Brown, and Beige.* These concerts were just another way that Ellington made audiences aware of the seriousness of jazz.

One of the most important jazz festivals of the 20th century took place annually in Newport, Rhode Island. Ellington's orchestra played there almost every year. These became another way for audiences to learn about Duke's music. The concerts were recorded, and sold millions of copies.

LATER YEARS: Ellington continued to compose and perform into his later years. He wrote religious music, too. His Sacred Concerts combined musical styles drawn from Africa, Europe, and America. These were performed in churches all over the world.

Ellington also composed music for ballet. In 1970, the American Ballet Theater commissioned him to write the music for a dance called *The River*. The choreographer was the great **Alvin Ailey.** Audiences loved the work. It is still performed by dance companies.

Duke Ellington died of lung cancer on May 24, 1974. He was mourned by millions. Thousands of people attended his funeral. It was the passing of one of the greatest musicians of the 20th century.

DUKE ELLINGTON'S HOME AND FAMILY: Ellington married his high school sweetheart, Edna Thompson, in 1918. They had one son, Mercer. Mercer took over the Ellington band after his father's death. He continued to lead the band until the 1990s. Mercer Ellington died in 1996.

HIS LEGACY: Ellington is considered one of the finest composers of the 20th century. His output was enormous: he wrote more than 2,000 songs in his 50-year career. His work is still popular, and still inspires, musicians today. Songs like "Sophisticated Ladies" and "Take the 'A' Train" are American classics.

Ellington's African-American heritage gave essence to every part of his music. "My men and my race are the inspiration of my work," he said. "I try to catch the character and mood and feeling of my people. The music of my race is something more than the American idiom. It is the result of our transplantation to American soil and was our reaction, in plantation days, to the life we lived. What we could not say openly we expressed in music. The characteristic, melancholic music of my race has been forged from the very white heat of our sorrows and from our gropings. I think the music of my race is something that is going to live, something which posterity will honor in a higher sense than merely that of the music of the ballroom."

WORLD WIDE WEB SITES:

http://dellington.org
http://www.americaslibrary.gov/cgi-bin/page.cgi/aa/ellington
http://www.pbs.org/jazz/biography/arits/_id_ellington_duke.htm
http://www.redhotjazz.com/duke.html

Ralph Ellison

1914 - 1994

African-American Novelist, Short Story Writer, and Essayist

Author of *Invisible Man*

RALPH ELLISON WAS BORN on March 1, 1914, in Oklahoma City, Oklahoma. His parents were Lewis and Ida Ellison. They named their first son Ralph Waldo Ellison, after the American poet Ralph Waldo Emerson. Lewis ran an ice and coal business. Ida was a domestic worker. Ralph had one brother, Herbert.

RALPH ELLISON GREW UP in Oklahoma City in a loving family. His neighborhood was integrated, and he had many white friends. Both his parents loved to read, and Ralph became an eager reader, too.

Tragically, Ralph's father died in an accident when Ralph was three. His mother worked hard to support her two sons. Ralph helped out, too, selling newspapers and working at a local drug store.

Ralph and his brother were raised without much money, but with great confidence in themselves. Their mother made sure they had chemistry and electricity sets and a toy typewriter. She brought home records and magazines from the homes she cleaned. She encouraged them to read, and to dream big dreams.

RALPH ELLISON WENT TO SCHOOL at the local public schools. He did well in school, and soon found one of the great loves of his life: music.

When Ralph was eight, his mother bought him a used cornet. He studied the horn, and he became a great player. At Douglass High School, Ralph played in the band and orchestra. As a teenager, he cut the grass of the conductor of the Oklahoma City Orchestra in exchange for lessons.

Ralph loved jazz and blues especially. While working at the local drugstore, he met many of the local black jazz musicians. They became his inspiration and source of what was new in the world of music.

Ellison did so well in school and music that he received a scholarship to Tuskegee Institute. That is an outstanding traditional black college in Alabama. He was so poor that he got to Tuskegee by riding a freight train. He studied composition for three years, pledging to write a symphony by the age of 26. Then his scholarship ran out. Ellison moved to New York, hoping to find work and make enough money to return to school.

LIFE IN NEW YORK: Ellison did many different odd jobs while living in New York. He did office work and fixed radios and record players. One day, he met the famous **HARLEM RENAISSANCE** poet **Langston Hughes** at the YMCA. He also got to know writer **Richard Wright**.

Wright was editing a magazine. He told Ellison to submit a book review. "My review was accepted and published," Ellison recalled. "I was hooked." He wrote a short story for the next issue, but the magazine failed before it was published.

In 1937, Ellison went to Dayton, Ohio, to care for his sick mother. After she died, he and his brother lived in poverty. They hunted wild birds to eat, sleeping in a car at night. Soon afterward, he returned to New York.

BECOMING A WRITER: Ellison had begun several stories by the time he got back to New York. This was during the Great Depression, when up to one-quarter of Americans couldn't find work. Ellison got a job as a researcher for the Federal Writers' Project. He collected folk tales from the black community. His job was to write them down for a history project on African-American culture.

After a few years with the Writers' Project, Ellison went off on his own as a writer. He published stories, essays, and book reviews. He helped edit *The Negro Quarterly*, a literary magazine. He also read all he could. He especially loved the poetry of T.S. Eliot and the novels of Ernest Hemingway. They became important influences on his work.

In 1943, during World War II, Ellison joined the Merchant Marine. He worked as a cook for two years, until he became ill after drinking polluted water. He left the Merchant Marine and moved to Vermont. There, he began to work on the book that would become his masterpiece.

INVISIBLE MAN: Ellison said that the novel's first line: "I am an invisible man," just came to him one day. It is one of the most famous first lines in American literature. The book is about a young African-American man trying to understand his place in the world. He wants to find meaning in his life, but he doesn't want to be defined by the color of his skin.

The narrator has no name. He has no identity. "I am invisible," he says, "because people refuse to see me." The young man grows up in the segregated South. He goes to college, and then to New York. He becomes involved in the fight for equal rights. But soon the true nature of race in America overwhelms him. People refuse to see him as anything other than a black man. The novel ends with the character angry, confused, and in despair.

The novel was a sensation when it first appeared. Ellison's powerful work raised issues about race in America that made people think. The story is woven with the folk tales he'd gathered, and the jazz music he loved. *Invisible Man* is one of most studied works of

American Literature. It is studied in high schools and colleges in the U.S. and around the world.

LATER CAREER: After the huge success of *Invisible Man*, Ellison published short stories and essays. He became a popular professor of literature and writing. He taught at several colleges, including New York University.

Ellison also worked on a second novel for the rest of his life. He never completed or published it. During the 1960s, his home in Massachusetts burned down. The manuscript for his second novel was destroyed. He tried to reconstruct it, but he left it as a 2,000 page manuscript when he died. His editor and friend John Callahan worked on the novel, and published a portion of it as *Juneteenth* in 1999.

RALPH ELLISON'S HOME AND FAMILY: Ellison married his wife, Fanny, in 1946. They were married for 48 years. They did not have children. The couple lived in an apartment in the Washington Heights section of New York City. Ralph Ellison died of cancer on April 16, 1994.

HIS LEGACY: Ellison is honored as the author of one of the most important novels of the 20th century. *Invisible Man* is a powerful exploration of race in America, but it is much more. It reaches out to people of all backgrounds, regardless of race or nationality. More than 50 years after its publication, its power still moves readers.

WORLD WIDE WEB SITES:

http://aalbc.com/authors/ellison.htm
http://www.pbs.org/wnet/americanmasters/dtatbase/ellison_r.html

Ella Fitzgerald

1917 - 1996

African-American Singer

"The First Lady of Song"

ELLA FITZGERALD WAS BORN on April 25, 1917, in Newport News, Virginia. Her parents were William and Temperance Fitzgerald. They never married, but they lived together for several years. Her father left the family when Ella was two years old.

Ella and her mother moved to New York when she was three. Later, her mother married a man named Joe Da Silva. They had a daughter, Frances, who was Ella's half-sister.

ELLA FITZGERALD GREW UP in Yonkers, just north of New York City. She grew up with all kinds of kids—Irish, Italian, Greek, and

African-American. She was a shy child, but she loved to sing and dance. And she knew that someday she'd be a star. "Someday you're going to see me in the headlines," she told a friend. "I'm going to be famous."

Ella started singing in the choir at church when she was in elementary school. She also started dancing with Charles Miller, the brother of her friend Annette Miller. They would make up dances and perform them for all the people of the neighborhood.

ELLA FITZGERALD WENT TO SCHOOL at the local public schools. She went to P.S. 10 in Yonkers for elementary school. Next, she attended Benjamin Franklin Junior High. She was an excellent student, and always loved singing and dancing. One friend remembered that during lunch break, Ella would stand outside the school, dancing. "She would be popping and shaking and swaying, dancing to herself," he recalled.

EARLY TRAGEDY: When Ella was just 15, her mother died. This was a dark, terrible time in her life. Her stepfather became abusive. She left home and went to live with an aunt. She dropped out of school to make money.

Fitzgerald got in trouble, and wound up in a juvenile detention center. The New York State Training School for Girls was a terrible place. She and the other African-American girls were kept in the basement. They were treated horribly. As soon as she was released, she went to New York City. She lived on the streets and made money anyway she could.

Then, on November 21, 1934, Ella Fitzgerald got her big break.

Fitzgerald performing in Stockholm, Sweden, Feb. 10, 1952.

A SPECIAL NIGHT AT THE APOLLO THEATER: On that date, Fitzgerald entered an amateur night contest at Harlem's famed Apollo Theater. She was supposed to compete as a dancer. Fitzgerald described her 15-year-old self:

"There I was, nervous as can be," she recalled. "Only 15 years old, with the skinniest legs you've ever seen. And I froze. I got cold feet. The man in charge said that I had better do something up there. So I said I wanted to sing instead."

She sang a song made popular by one of her favorite singers, Connee Boswell. It was "The Object of My Affection." The audience went wild. She won the $25 prize. More importantly, one of the greatest careers in music was launched that night.

A LEGENDARY CAREER: Fitzgerald's singing career lasted more than 60 years. She sang in many different styles over those years, from Big Band, to jazz, bebop, and pop. She brought her own gifts to all those types of music. She had an unfailing sense of phrasing, knowing how to bring out the meaning behind the notes and words. She could take apart the rhythm and melodic line of a piece of music, rework it, and make it her own. Her sense of pitch was unwavering, too. She could hit a note right in the middle, never off key.

Fitzgerald's career took off in 1935, when her friend and fellow musician Charles Linton introduced her to Chick Webb. Webb was the leader of a well-known Big Band.

The Big Band Era: The Big Band era of the 1930s and 1940s was named for full orchestras that played popular tunes. It's often called "swing" music, because its tunes and rhythms are great for dancing. The groups often had a major composer, like **Duke Ellington**, as the leader.

Fitzgerald toured the country with Webb's band. They were hugely popular. She started to make records, too. In 1938, she had her first million-seller, "A-Tisket, A-Tasket," a song she co-wrote with Al Feldman.

When Webb died in 1939, Fitzgerald became the head of the band. They toured for several years, and made records together.

Fitzgerald performing with Duke Ellington, January 28, 1966.

By then, she was performing as the featured singer with other Big Bands.

Jazz and "Scat" Singing: In the 1940s, Fitzgerald began to develop her gift for jazz singing. She learned to take apart a melody and improvise small solos. She also began to improvise and sing nonsense syllables to tunes. That's what "scat" singing is. Scat was probably created by **Louis Armstrong**, but Ella was one of the best scatters ever.

Bebop: In the 1940s, jazz greats **Dizzie Gillespie** and **Charlie Parker** created a new direction in jazz with a style called bebop. Unlike the music of the Big Bands, bebop was music to *listen* to, not to dance to. It's full of complex chords and unusual harmonies. Bebop explores the harmonic possibilities, especially in chord progressions, rather than the melodic qualities of a song.

Fitzgerald performed bebop with Gillespie, and the results were fantastic. She loved it, too. "I used to get thrilled listening to him when he did his bebop."

Norman Granz: In 1953, Fitzgerald met the record producer Norman Granz. He became her manager, and helped produce the records that made her world-famous.

Granz developed the performance and recording careers of Fitzgerald and other African-American jazz artists. He started a series of famous live concerts from the Los Angeles Philharmonic. These concerts were recorded and broadcast all over the country. They introduced a generation of listeners to some of the finest jazz musicians, including Fitzgerald. Granz also refused to abide by the segregated seating in the South. He made sure that all the concerts he booked allowed African-Americans the best seats in the house.

Granz helped make Fitzgerald one of the greatest recording artists ever. Over the years, she made more than 70 record albums that sold millions of copies. Under Granz's management, Fitzgerald explored some of the greatest music ever created in America.

The "Songbooks": With Granz, Fitzgerald recorded songs by some of the finest composers of the era. These recordings became her "Songbook" series. Her versions of the music of **Duke Ellington**, Cole Porter, Ira and George Gershwin, and others became classic collections. They were enjoyed by jazz lovers and general listeners, too.

Fitzgerald performing at Carnegie Hall, New York City, June 25, 1989.

Fitzgerald's fellow musicians admired her ability as much as her millions of fans. One of them was Ed Thigpen, who played drums for her for years. "Ella's musicianship is just incredible," he said. "Playing with her is like playing with a full orchestra. She has a vast knowledge of every song ever written, knowing all the verses, knowing what songs mean, and still interpreting them her own way. Her rhythmic sense is uncanny."

In the 1960s, Fitzgerald's audience grew as she appeared on television specials. Her fame grew around the world, as she continued to tour and record.

HEALTH PROBLEMS: In the late 1970s, Fitzgerald's health began to fail. She had diabetes. That disease can cause problems with the heart, circulation, and eyes. She began to lose her eyesight, and she had to have heart surgery. She performed for the last time in

1993. Ella Fitzgerald died after a stroke on June 15, 1996. She was mourned, and praised, by fans the world over.

ELLA FITZGERALD'S HOME AND FAMILY: Fitzgerald was married two times. She married her first husband, Benny Kornegay, in 1941. They divorced a year later.

In 1947, Fitzgerald married the famous bass player Ray Brown. They adopted the son of Fitzgerald's sister, and renamed him Ray Brown Jr. Fitzgerald and Brown divorced in 1953, but they remained good friends and performed together for years. After her death, Brown arranged a musical tribute to her at Carnegie Hall.

HER LEGACY: Ella Fitzgerald was known worldwide as the "First Lady of Song." She was one of the finest interpreters of some of the finest songs of the 20th century. She brought the joy of her music to millions, introducing many to the rhythms of jazz and bebop. She is an American treasure, influencing generations of musicians and inspiring music lovers everywhere.

WORLD WIDE WEB SITES:

http://lcweb2.loc.gov/diglib/ihas/loc/natlib.scdb.200033594/
http://www.loc.gov/loc/lcib/9708/ella.html
http://www.pbs.org/wnet/americanmasters/database/fitzgerald_e.html

Marvin Gaye
1939 - 1984
African-American Singer, Songwriter, and Musician Creator of the Hit Songs "What's Going On?" and "I Heard It through the Grapevine"

MARVIN GAYE WAS BORN on April 2, 1939, in Washington, D.C. His full name was originally Marvin Pentz Gay Jr. He added the *e* to his last name when he launched his music career. Marvin's parents were Alberta Cooper Gay and Marvin Pentz Gay Sr. His mother worked as a maid. His father was a minister. Marvin had an older sister, Jeanne, a younger brother, Frankie, and a younger sister, Zeola.

MARVIN GAYE GREW UP in a rough, all-black neighborhood in the nation's capital. His parents were deeply religious. They belonged to the Seventh-Day Adventist Church. They expected their children to spend every weekend studying religion and worshipping God.

Marvin had trouble following his parents' strict rules. He never got along well with his father. Marvin Sr. was a difficult man who sometimes beat his children. "Living with my father was like living with a king, a very peculiar, changeable, cruel, and all-powerful king," Marvin remembered.

When Marvin was three years old, he started singing gospel music at church. He learned to play the organ a few years later. People at church told him that he had a natural talent for music. Marvin loved playing and listening to music. Music gave him a way to escape from his difficult childhood.

MARVIN GAYE WENT TO SCHOOL at the public schools in his neighborhood. He learned to play drums, piano, and guitar at Cardozo High School. In 1957 Marvin dropped out of school and joined the U.S. Air Force. But he did not handle military discipline very well. He got released from the Air Force within a year.

BREAKING INTO THE MUSIC BUSINESS: After returning home, Gaye decided to start a career in music. He and some friends formed a band called the Marquees. They played some concerts for high-school students. They also released a single of one of their songs, but the record didn't sell well.

Luckily for Gaye, he met a record promoter named Harvey Fuqua. Fuqua asked Gaye to join his band, the Moonglows. In 1959 they recorded a hit song, "Ten Commandments of Love." At this point Gaye added an *e* to his last name. He did it partly to distance himself from his father. He also felt that the new name seemed more serious and manly.

MOTOWN RECORDS: In 1960 Gaye moved to Detroit, Michigan. An African-American businessman named **Berry Gordy** had just started a company called Motown Records there. Gaye became a backup singer and musician for Smokey Robinson and other well-known Motown acts. He also married Gordy's sister, Anna. Since Anna was 17 years older than Gaye, some people said he married her to advance his career.

Gaye soon earned a chance to be a solo artist for Motown. In 1961 he released his first album, *The Soulful Moods of Marvin Gaye.* It was not very successful. Most of the songs on the album were slow and had a jazz sound.

People at Motown Records encouraged Gaye to change his style. They wanted him to play faster rhythm-and-blues (R&B) songs. This type of music was popular with young audiences. Gaye agreed to make the change. By 1964 he had placed several songs on *Billboard* magazine's list of the most popular records in the country. Gaye's early R&B hits included "Can I Get a Witness," "Pride and Joy," and "How Sweet It Is (to Be Loved by You)."

DUETS WITH TAMMI TERRELL: Gaye's good looks helped him win over many female fans. Motown decided to take advantage of his appeal. The company arranged for him to sing romantic duets with top female artists. Gaye's favorite partner was a young singer named Tammi Terrell. They recorded three successful albums together. Many of their songs were big hits, like "Ain't No Mountain High Enough" and "Ain't Nothing Like the Real Thing."

Sadly, Terrell collapsed on stage during a 1967 concert. Doctors learned that she had a brain tumor. She died in 1970 at age 24. Gaye took her death very hard. He became depressed and abused drugs. His marriage started to fall apart.

Gaye performing, 1966.

Gaye refused to perform in concert for years after Terrell died. But he continued working in the recording studio. In 1968 he had his first number- one hit record, "I Heard It through the Grapevine." Its tone was very dark and moody compared to most Motown songs. The next year Gaye released another album, *MPG.* Most of the songs on this album talked about the problems in his personal life.

CHANGING DIRECTION: The United States went through a number of important changes during the 1960s and 1970s. African-Americans fought for equality in the **CIVIL RIGHTS MOVEMENT**. Many Americans protested against the country's involvement in the Vietnam War. Gaye started to feel bad about recording love songs during such troubled times. He wanted to make music that talked about the social and political issues facing the nation.

Gaye wrote a whole album's worth of songs about problems like war, poverty, racism, and pollution. He was one of the first black musicians to address these issues. Motown did not want to

Gaye performing in New York City, May 1983.

release the album at first. Berry Gordy worried that listeners would not like what Gaye had to say.

The record company finally agreed to release *What's Going On?* in 1971. The album became a huge success with both fans and music critics. Many listeners connected with the anti-war message of the title song, "What's Going On?" Many others shared the concerns about pollution Gaye expressed in "Mercy Mercy Me (the Ecology)." Critics praised the singer for expanding the boundaries of R&B music. Before long, other Motown artists started covering important issues in their songs.

The album helped Gaye earn a Trendsetter of the Year Award from *Billboard* and an Image Award from the **NATIONAL ASSOCIATION FOR THE ADVANCEMENT OF COLORED PEOPLE (NAACP).**

TROUBLES CONTINUE: Gaye switched musical directions again in 1973. He released an album of love songs called *Let's Get It On.* It became the best-selling album of his career.

In the meantime, Gaye continued to have problems in his personal life. He started having an affair with Janis Hunter, the 17-year-old daughter of a jazz musician. He divorced his wife in 1975 and married Hunter in 1977. They had two children together. But the marriage failed after a couple of years.

Gaye struggled with depression and drug addiction. He also ran out of money and got in trouble for not paying his taxes. In 1979 he moved to Hawaii and lived in a van. Later he tried to escape his problems by moving to Europe.

In 1981 Gaye left Motown Records and signed a contract with CBS Records. The next year he released his final album, *Midnight Love*. The most popular song on the album was "Sexual Healing." It was the number-one song in America for four months. The album won two Grammy Awards.

In 1983 Gaye sang on the TV broadcast of the Grammys and on Motown's 25th Anniversary Special. These were his last public appearances. Gaye's personal problems got worse. He was treated in a hospital for drug addiction. He also threatened to commit suicide. Gaye ended up moving in with his parents in Los Angeles, California. He and his father had violent arguments.

A TRAGIC DEATH: On April 1, 1984, the singer was shot and killed by his father. The two men had been fighting about money. Gaye would have turned 45 the following day. His father claimed that he had acted in self-defense. Doctors later learned that Marvin Sr. had a brain tumor. He did not have to go to jail for killing his son.

Music fans everywhere mourned the tragic loss of Marvin Gaye. More than 10,000 people attended his funeral in Los Angeles.

Gaye with son Frankie, June 1980.

Many famous singers performed at the funeral, including **Stevie Wonder.** In 1987 Gaye was inducted into the Rock and Roll Hall of Fame. He was selected for his contributions to soul and R&B music as a singer, songwriter, producer, and musician.

MARVIN GAYE'S HOME AND FAMILY: Gaye was married and divorced twice. His first wife was Anna Gordy. They adopted a son, Marvin Jr. His second wife was Janis Hunter. They had two children together: a son, Frankie, and a daughter, Nona. Before his death, Gaye lived in Los Angeles, California.

HIS LEGACY: Gaye is remembered as one of the most important and innovative R & B musicians of the 20th century. His songs touched people of all ages and backgrounds. He once said, "I felt the strong urge to write music and to write lyrics that would touch the souls of men." He did that, in songs that will endure for generations.

WORLD WIDE WEB SITES:

http://www.rockhall.com/inductee/marvin_gaye
http://www.rollingstone.com/artists/marvingaye/biography
http://www.history-of-rock.com/marvin_gaye.htm

Savion Glover
1973 -
African-American Tap Dancer and Choreographer
Creator of *Bring in 'da Noise, Bring in 'da Funk*

SAVION GLOVER WAS BORN on November 19, 1973, in Newark, New Jersey. His name is pronounced SAY-vee-on GLOV-er. His unusual first name was created by his mother, Yvette Glover. She based it on the word "savior." Yvette is a singer and actress. Savion's father left the family when he was little, and has not kept in contact. Savion has two younger brothers, Carlton and Abron.

SAVION GLOVER GREW UP in a poor section of Newark. The family lived in a housing project with other poor families, where some kids turn to crime. Savion says it would have been easy for him to turn out like that, too. "I would probably be stealing your car or selling drugs right now. I got friends who do that, but tap saved me."

Savion had many relatives who were musicians, and he grew up surrounded with music. His grandmother and grandfather were singers, and so was his mom. When Savion was just a baby, his grandmother picked him up and hummed to him. He looked up at her, smiled, and hummed right back at her. It was amazing. Most kids can't understand and follow a tune when they're that little. But Savion could.

From the time he was a toddler, Savion would take knives and forks and beat on the table, pans, walls, anything to make a rhythm. That urge to make a beat, to create patterns in sound, would be with him for the rest of his life.

Savion's mom started him in violin lessons at four. He liked it, but he really wanted to play the drums. So he switched to drums, and his drum teacher couldn't get over how well he played. The teacher told Savion's mom that he should go to a special school for musicians. So at the age of four, Savion auditioned at the Newark Community School of the Arts. He was accepted and became the youngest scholarship student ever.

STARTING TO DANCE: At the age of seven, Savion started taking lessons at the Broadway Dance Center in New York City. He remembers his first day of tap dance class very well.

"My mom couldn't afford dance shoes, so she put me in these old cowboy boots with a hard bottom so I could get some sound out. I used them for seven months. When I finally got real tap

Glover, center, and fellow cast members from "Bring in 'da Noise, Bring in 'da Funk."

shoes, I was nervous. I kept moving my feet, thinking, 'Oh, so this is how it's supposed to sound'."

But regardless of his shoes, Savion had found what he loved. He remembers that he practiced "everywhere." "I would dance waiting for a cab, walking, in the shower." When he was eight, his mom took him to see two great tap dancers, Chuck Green and Lon Chaney, perform. After that, his mind was set. "Mommy, this is what I want to do," he told her.

FIRST ROLES: When Savion was 10, he auditioned for a Broadway show, *The Tap Dance Kid.* He got the role as the understudy for the lead. (An "understudy" is the person who fills in when an actor is ill or on vacation). One year later, the lead left the show, and Savion became the star.

Savion's dancing was a sensation. Audiences loved him, and he loved being in show business. But he had a normal life, too. He says that during those early years, his mom made sure he had time for himself. "She made it possible for me to chill out, have my life, be a kid, grow up."

Glover's next big role was in *Black and Blue*. The show is based on the great African-American tappers and musicians of the 1930s and 1940s. What he learned helped him to develop his own style of tap.

SAVION GLOVER'S DANCE STYLE: Glover's dance style is known as "rhythm tap." It is based on using the whole foot to make the sounds and beat patterns of tap. The other style is known as "Broadway," or show tap. In that style, the dancer mainly uses the ball and heel of the foot.

Glover says his style is more expressive. He uses all parts of his foot, making rhythms that sound like they come from a drum. "Tap is like a drum solo," he says. "I believe you can get so many tones out of using your foot. Your heel is like your bass drum. The ball of your foot is the snare. The side is like a rim shot. A regular tap dancer knows ball and heel. He doesn't know about the side of your arch, the side of your foot. We get sounds from the pinkie toe to all sides of the foot, back to the heel."

"Drummers carry around their sticks," says Glover. "We carry around our tap shoes." And he has amazing shoes. His feet are

Gregory Hines, left, and Glover performing together.

big—he wears a size 12½ dance shoe. To add more sound, he has his shoes made with extra metal.

Glover's dancing is fast and loud. He's got long dreadlocks that fly around as he moves like lightening across the stage. His feet move so fast, they sound like drums and hammers all at once. He goes up on his toes, then back on his heels, always moving. Audiences everywhere, all over the world, love him.

LEARNING FROM THE MASTERS: In developing his style, Glover worked with some of the greatest tappers of all time. He danced with legends like Gregory Hines, Diane Walker, Jimmy Slyde, and Sammy Davis Jr. From them, he learned the moves and the rhythms.

It's a style sometimes called "hoofing." Glover says it's "dancing from the waist down. People think tap dancing is all arms and legs and this big old smile. No. It's raw. It's real. It's rhythm. It's us. It's ours."

In learning from the old hoofers, Glover also learned to "improvise." A dancer would take a step, then create a whole new move. So he was actually creating new movements, new steps, new ways of dancing.

In 1989, Glover appeared with Gregory Hines in the movie *Tap*. One scene shows them doing a "challenge dance." The "challenge dance" is a big part of rhythm tap. The dancers try to one-up each other with dazzling moves.

JELLY'S LAST JAM: Glover and Hines appeared together again in 1992. They starred in *Jelly's Last Jam*, a tribute to the music of Jelly Roll Morton. Morton was a famous black jazz musician from the 1920s and 1930s. The show was a hit, and Savion Glover was a star.

SESAME STREET: From 1991 to 1995, Glover was also a regular actor on *Sesame Street*. He played a dancer named Savion. He got to teach other actors, and Muppets, to dance. He says that Snuffleupagus was the hardest to teach—"he has four feet!" says Glover. "Elmo's my favorite. He's always finding out something new, kind of like me."

FITTING IN SCHOOL WORK: Glover went to several different schools over the years. He started out at a Catholic school in Newark. But when his dancing career took off, he had a tutor. Later, he attended the Professional Children's School and the East Harlem Performing Arts High School. While working full time as a

Glover and Hoots the Owl on "Sesame Street."

dancer, Glover received his high school degree from Newark's Arts High School.

BRING IN 'DA NOISE, BRING IN 'DA FUNK: In the early 1990s, Glover began to choreograph—to create dances. He worked with director George C. Wolfe to create a show called *Bring in 'da Noise, Bring in 'da Funk*. It's a tribute to the history of African-American music and dancing. The tone is sometimes sad, and sometimes joyful. He's showing all of black American life, from slavery to the problems of today. He uses all kinds of music, too, from spirituals to jazz to hip-hop. Glover used hip-hop dance moves, too, adding another style to his own.

IMPROVOGRAPHY: One of Glover recent shows is called "improvography." It's a word Gregory Hines made up to describe the combination of improvising and choreography. In the show's first half, Glover dances a solo that he improvises every night. He sings, too, and appears on stage with several jazz musicians who accompany him. The second half features Glover dancing with members of his dance company, called Ti Dii (pronounced "tie dye").

OTHER PROJECTS: Glover continues to dance, travel, and teach. He's also created dance pieces set to the music of great classical composers, like Vivaldi, Bach, and Mendelssohn.

HAPPY FEET: In 2006, Glover's *dancing* appeared in the hit movie *Happy Feet.* In what is called "motion capture performance," motion sensors were attached to Glover's body. Then, as he danced like a penguin, a computer picked up his steps and turned them into the digital movement you see on the screen. Glover thought it was great. He even enjoyed learning to walk like a penguin.

INFLUENCES: Glover often talks about what he learned from older tap dancers. He's especially grateful to Gregory Hines, Diane Walker, Jimmy Slyde, and Sammy Davis Jr.

"My biggest influence has been the great dancers who raised me, took me under their wings, taught me everything I know. They allowed me to imitate them until I had my own style."

SAVION GLOVER'S HOME AND FAMILY: Glover is married with a son named Chaney (in honor of one of the great tappers). He and his family live in New York City. He's still very close to his mom, and a few years ago bought her a home in New Jersey.

HIS LEGACY: Glover is one of the greatest tap dancers of his generation. He will continue to inspire audiences for years to come, with his message of the importance of dance to life. "Tap is joyful, it's fun, it can make you very happy. It is also a serious discipline and can express lots of feelings and thoughts. Some are sad, some blue, some angry, some thoughtful. And what I received I love giving back. I love to teach, to work with youngsters."

WORLD WIDE WEB SITES:

http://broadwaydancecenter.com
http://www.js-interactive.com/savion/
http://www.tapdance.org

Berry Gordy Jr.

1929 -

African-American Songwriter, Recording Executive, and Entrepreneur

Founder of Motown Records

BERRY GORDY JR. WAS BORN on November 28, 1929, in Detroit, Michigan. He was the seventh of eight children born to Bertha and Berry Gordy Sr. His father was a carpenter and plasterer and his mother sold insurance and real estate. They also ran a grocery store and a print shop. These very hard working parents raised all eight children to be ambitious and to try new things.

BERRY GORDY GREW UP in Detroit. The Gordys were a close and musical family who all helped each other in many ways. As a young boy Berry had two loves: music and boxing. He spent his time writing songs on the piano and training at a Detroit gym.

BERRY GORDY WENT TO SCHOOL at the local public schools. He dropped out of school to became a professional lightweight boxer when he was 19. He soon discovered how tough the life of a boxer was and decided to spend all his time writing songs. He started sending his songs to contests in hopes of winning.

BEFORE MOTOWN: In 1951, Gordy was drafted into the army. While serving there he took classes and earned his high school equivalency diploma (GED).

When he got out of the army, Gordy began working on an auto assembly line. In 1953 he married Thelma Coleman. In 1954 their first child was born, a daughter they named Hazel Joy. They had two more children, Berry III and Terry.

BEGINNING A CAREER IN MUSIC: While working at the auto factory Gordy continued to write songs and send them to contests, magazines and singers. In 1955 he received a loan from his family to open a record store called the 3-D Record Mart. Although the store didn't stay open long it was Gordy's first attempt at making a living from music.

BIG BREAK: In 1957, a song written by Gordy, his sister Gwen, and Tyran Carlo was recorded by Jackie Wilson. The song, *Reet Petite*, was Wilson's first hit. It made Berry Gordy $1,000.

During the next two years Gordy co-wrote four more songs for Jackie Wilson. He also spent time scouting for more singers. In 1957 Gordy went to an audition held by Wilson. He heard a group led by William "Smokey" Robinson. At the audition, Robinson's group was rejected for sounding too much like other popular groups. But Gordy was impressed by the original material the group sang. He introduced himself as a songwriter. This was the beginning of a life-long relationship between Smokey Robinson and Berry Gordy.

By 1958 Gordy was becoming discouraged because he was not making much money from his song writing. He decided to form his own publishing company so he could have more control over his songs and the money they made. The company was named "Jobete." It was named for his three children: Hazel Joy (jo), Berry (be), and Terry (te). Gordy was also unhappy with the way his songs were being produced. It was time for him to form his own corporation.

THE TAMLA RECORD LABEL: In 1959, with an $800 loan from his family, Berry Gordy took control of his songs and established his own record label, Tamla. With six employees and an apartment on Gladstone Street in Detroit, they put together and released a song by Marv Johnson. It was a mid-sized hit. Later that year, Marv Johnson's "You've Got What it Takes" became the first song of Gordy's to make it into the Top 10.

Gordy bought a house on West Grand Boulevard in Detroit and named it "Hitsville USA." This became home to the Tamla label. It was also a recording studio and a favorite hang out for young Detroit musicians.

MOTOWN: In 1960 Gordy created a second record label. This one was called Motown. The roots of the music were in urban rhythm and blues. But Gordy wanted to appeal to all young people, not

Gordy receiving the NAACP Award of the Year from Barry Greg, Sept. 27, 1968.

just African-Americans. The early advertising slogan was "The Sound of Young America."

In 1960 the first song completely written by Gordy and produced at Hitsville, "Money (That's What I Want)" became a hit. When Smokey Robinson and the Miracles hit with "Way Over There" and "Shop Around," Gordy and Motown became known across the United States.

EARLY TALENT: With the success of Smokey Robinson and the Miracles, hundreds of young, talented artists began showing up at Hitsville. Soon the Motown label was releasing songs by **Marvin Gaye**, the Temptations, the Supremes, the Four Tops, Martha and the Vandellas, Mary Wells, and **Stevie Wonder**.

A fantastic group of musicians backed up the singers on almost every Motown recording made in the 1960s. The Funk Brothers included a bass player, a drummer, a guitarist and a keyboard player. The musicians were paid between $25,000 and $50,000 dollars a year to stay with Motown. They were at the heart of the distinctive music that was quickly becoming recognized as the Motown Sound.

During the early 1960s Gordy's company had hit after hit. He was breaking the color barrier as he had hoped to do and the Motown sound was heard not just on black radio stations but pop (mainly white) radio stations as well.

To give his singers extra "polish," Gordy hired Maxine Powell to run the Motown Finishing School. She helped a generation of Motown artists look, speak and act like "stars."

THE MOTOWN SOUND: The year 1964 was an amazing one for Motown. Four of the company's five recordings went to #1. In 1965, five Motown releases reached #1. Gordy's eye and ear for talent and his decision to surround himself with creative people made Motown a music factory that produced hit after hit.

At the end of the 1960s a new group from Gary, Indiana, was brought to Gordy's attention. The Jackson 5 were signed to Motown and four of their first six singles reached #1 on the pop charts.

MOVING WEST: In 1966 Motown established a West Coast office in Los Angeles. Gordy wanted to expand Motown to include recording, films, television, and publishing. From the six employees on

Gordy receives his star on the Hollywood Walk of Fame, Oct. 29, 1996. Left to right: Stevie Wonder, Johnny Grant, Otis Williams, Gordy, Smokey Robinson, and Diana Ross.

Gladstone Street in Detroit, Motown had become a huge entertainment corporation.

Diana Ross of the Supremes was now Gordy's main star and he started grooming her for movies and TV. In 1968, Motown's first TV special, *TCB: Taking Care of Business,* featured the Supremes and the Temptations. In 1971 Diana Ross starred in her own TV special, called *Diana.*

LEAVING DETROIT: In June 1972 the Detroit offices of Motown were closed and all operations moved to Los Angeles. This probably made sense as Gordy was concentrating on making movies and TV specials. Many Motown fans, however, believed the move changed the heart and soul of Motown. For them, the most creative days were over.

MOVIES AND TELEVISION: In 1972 Motown made the leap to movie production. Diana Ross appeared in her first film role, playing Billie Holiday in *Lady Sings the Blues.* She won an Academy Award nomination for her performance.

Gordy's debut as a film director came in 1975 with *Mahogany,* starring Diana Ross. This was followed in 1978 by *The Wiz.* Although neither of these films did as well as *Lady Sings the Blues,* Motown (and Gordy) had established themselves as part of the film industry.

An NBC television special in 1983, *Motown 25—Yesterday, Today and Tomorrow* featured reunions of many of the early Motown groups. It included the Jackson 5, the Miracles, Marvin Gaye, and the Supremes. TV viewers loved it. It was the most-watched TV variety special in the history of television. The show, a tribute to Berry Gordy, won nine Emmy nominations

In 1975 another TV special brought awards to Motown. *Motown Returns to the Apollo* was filmed at the famous Apollo Theater in Harlem on its 50th anniversary. It later won an Emmy for the best variety, musical or comedy program.

During the early 80s Motown continued to sell thousands of albums. Lionel Richie and the Commodores were now on board and songs from Stevie Wonder and Marvin Gaye were reaching the Top Ten.

By the mid-80s, however, Motown was losing millions of dollars. Berry Gordy did what he never thought he could do. He sold Motown to the MCA recording company for $61 million. Although many old Motown fans were saddened by the sale, it was proof of Gordy's success. He had taken an $800 loan and built Motown into a multi-million dollar company.

Gordy with Smokey Robinson and Martha Reeves in front of Hitsville, U.S.A., Oct. 19, 2007.

BERRY GORDY'S HOME AND FAMILY: Gordy was married three times. His first wife was Thelma Coleman. They had three children, Hazel Joy, Berry III, and Terry, before they divorced in 1959. He married Raymona Singleton in 1960. They divorced in 1962. They had one son, Kennedy. His third wife was Grace Easton. They were married from 1990 to 1993.

HIS LEGACY: The Motown sound is Berry Gordy's legacy. The label will always be remembered for the many hits it produced in the 1960s. In fact, Motown produced more Top Ten hits than any other record label of the 1960s. The teenagers who grew up listening to Motown are older now, but they still love the music, as do a new generation of listeners.

Gordy is also noted for his charity work. He believes that education is the key to success, and established a fundraiser, the

Sterling Ball. It raises money for scholarships for inner city high school graduates. This event has helped hundreds of young men and women, black and white, continue their education in college. It was begun as a memorial to Berry's sister, Loucye Gordy Wakefield, who had been the first vice-president of Motown.

WORLD WIDE WEB SITES

http://www.bsnpubs.com/gordystory.html
http://www.history-of-rock.com/motown_records.htm
http://www.music.com/artist/gordy

Alex Haley
1921 - 1992
African-American Author and Creator of *Roots*

ALEX HALEY WAS BORN on August 11, 1921, in Ithaca, New York. His parents were Simon and Bertha Haley. When Alex was born, Simon was a college student and Bertha was a teacher. Alex had two younger brothers, George and Julius.

ALEX HALEY GREW UP with his maternal grandparents—his mother's parents. He and his mother lived with her family in Henning, Tennessee, while his father finished college. Both his parents stressed the importance of education. His mother was the first person in her family to attend college. His father worked his way through school, mostly at low-paying jobs.

While working as a railroad porter, his father met a man who changed the course of the family's fortunes. He was named R.S.M. Boyce. Simon Haley told Boyce about his dreams, and his plans to achieve them. Boyce was so impressed with Simon that he paid his college tuition in full.

That act of generosity allowed Simon to complete both college and graduate school. He became a professor at Alabama A & M. The family was reunited, and enjoyed a prosperous life together. Haley remembered it all his life. "Instead of being raised on a sharecrop farm, we grew up in a home with educated parents, shelves full of books, and with pride in ourselves."

THE ROOTS OF *ROOTS*: While growing up on his grandparents' farm, Haley first heard the stories that would become the center of his life's work. His grandmother and great aunts loved to tell him stories of his ancestors. One, whom they called "The African," was named "Kintay." He had been brought to this country as a slave in the 18th century.

Haley remembered the experience vividly. "There in the summer early evenings, my grandmother and her sisters used to sit in their rocking chairs on the front porch. Night after night, they'd reminisce about our family members who had been slaves in somewhere called Alamance County, North Carolina. They were freed by the Civil War and came in a wagon train led by grandma's grandpa."

These fascinating stories would become real to Alex in a way he could never imagine.

ALEX HALEY WENT TO SCHOOL at the local public schools. He didn't do terribly well in school, but he loved to read and was a good writer, too. He graduated from high school at 15 and went to Elizabeth City Teachers College. After two years there, he decided to leave school.

JOINING THE COAST GUARD: In 1939, at the age of 18, Haley joined the U.S. Coast Guard. That branch of the armed services protects the coastal waters of the nation. He spent 20 years with the Coast Guard, as a sailor.

Haley was able to use his writing skills right away. He had a series of writing jobs for the Coast Guard. He wrote articles for Coast Guard newsletters and magazines. He had a sideline job, too. Haley wrote love letters for his fellow sailors, charging $1 each.

Haley started writing articles for general magazines, too. When he retired from the Coast Guard, in 1959, he started to make his living as a writer.

WRITING CAREER: Haley struggled for several years, trying to make enough money as a writer. It was tough. He remembered he was "down to 18 cents and two cans of sardines. A friend called with the offer of a job in the civil service. I turned him down."

Finally, a writing job came his way. It allowed him to continue as a writer. But Haley never forgot how desperate he'd gotten. He framed those two cans of sardines. They hung on the wall of his Tennessee home for years.

Haley began to publish a series of in-depth interviews with leading figures. One of them was Malcolm X, the fiery political leader. (You can read a profile of Malcolm X in *Biography for Beginners: African-American Leaders, Vol. 1.*)

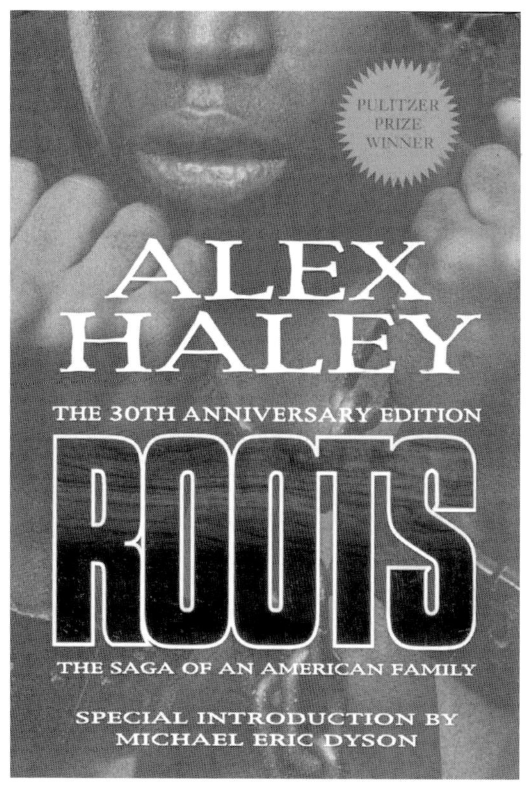

THE AUTOBIOGRAPHY OF MALCOLM X: Haley decided to expand the interview into a full-length book. When it was published in 1965, *The Autobiography of Malcolm X* was a sensation. Tragically, it came out several months after Malcolm X's assassination. Yet it continues to be read, and it launched Haley's career.

A JOURNEY INTO THE PAST: After the success of the *Autobiography*, Haley turned to his own background. He began a 12-year search into his past, inspired by the stories he'd heard growing up. He started at the National Archives in Washington, D.C. He was trying to find out anything he could about his ancestor, "Kintay." He spent 6,500 hours doing research and consulted 1,000 records in over 50 libraries. All that hard work led him to the village of Juffure, in Gambia, West Africa.

In Juffure, Haley searched for the local "griot" (GREE-oh). Haley described griots as "almost living archives." These men are "trained from boyhood to memorize, preserve, and recite the centuries-old histories of villages, clans, family, great kings, holy men, and heroes."

Haley found the griot who knew the history of his family—Kintay, or "Kinte," in the local language. In retelling the Kinte history, the griot came to the point where Haley's personal history and his African heritage came together. The griot told how the eldest son of Omoro and Binta Kinte, named Kunta, "went away from this village to chop wood. And he was never seen again."

Haley couldn't believe it. "I felt as if I were carved out of rock," he recalled. "What that old man in back-country Africa had just uttered dovetailed with the very words my grandmother had always spoken during my boyhood on a porch in Tennessee." She'd heard the story "from her father, Tom, who had heard it from his father, George, who had heard it from his mother, Kizzy, who had been told by her father, the man who called himself Kintay. He had been out, not far from his village, chopping wood, intending to make a drum, when he had been set upon by four men, and kidnapped into slavery."

ROOTS: Over the next several years, Haley transformed his family history into *Roots*. Haley called the book "faction." It was a blend of "fact" and "fiction," based on all he had learned about his family history. *Roots* appeared first as a book, then as one of the most-watched television series of all time.

Roots tells the story of seven generations of the Haley family. It starts with the birth of Kunta Kinte and continues to the 1990s. It begins with the story of Kunta, relating how he is brought by force to the United States aboard a slave ship. Haley chronicles the brutality and horror of Kunta's life. He is sold to a Virginia slave owner, who names him Toby. Kunta refuses to accept his new

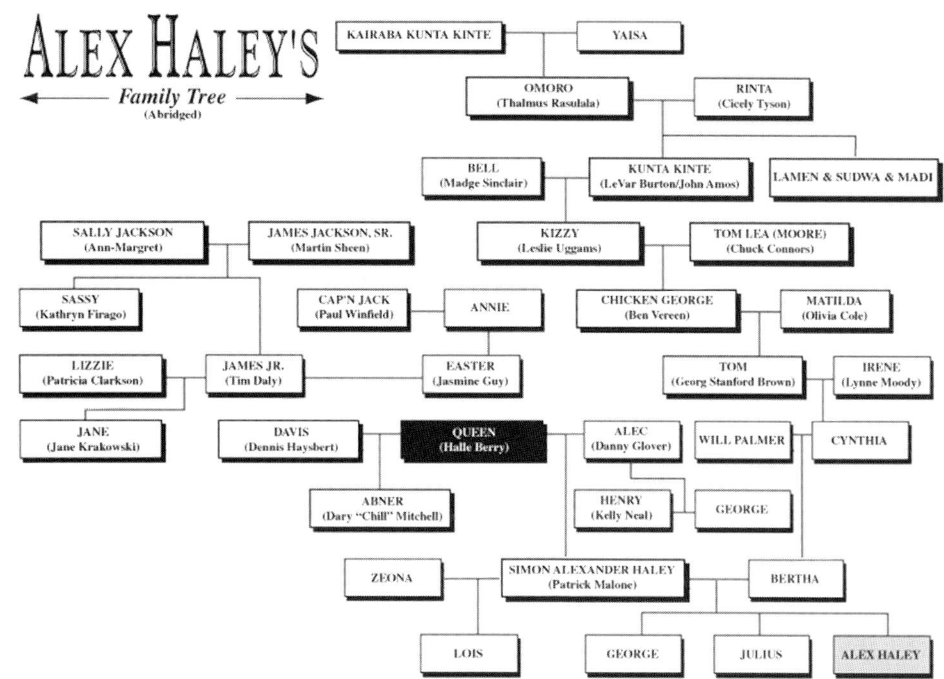

Haley family tree, indicating cast who portrayed family members in the TV adaptations based on Roots.

name. He tries to run away, and has a part of his foot cut off as punishment.

Kunta remains defiant, refusing to accept life as a slave. He raises his children to take pride in their African heritage. He teaches them to treasure, preserve, and pass on to later generations the true origins and honor of the Kinte clan. *Roots* chronicles the generations of Kintes through the nineteenth century, the Civil War, to the scenes of young Alex hearing about Kunta Kinte.

When *Roots* appeared in 1976, it was a sensation. The book sold millions of copies. Haley won many important awards, including the Pulitzer Prize and the National Book Award. But it was the television version of Haley's book that brought his story to millions of people worldwide.

***ROOTS* AND TELEVISION HISTORY:** *Roots* appeared as one of the first TV mini-series, in January 1977. The show's producers thought that a series about African-Americans wouldn't interest general audiences. How wrong they were.

More than 130 million viewers watched the eight episodes of *Roots*. It was one of the top-rated TV shows of all time. Americans thrilled to Haley's story of his ancestors. The cast featured some of the finest African-American actors of the time. It included LeVar Burton, John Amos, Ben Vereen, and Danny Glover.

Roots also inspired people of all backgrounds to research their own family histories. People all over the country began to trace their ancestry through public records. They researched birth, marriage, and death records. They reviewed passenger immigration lists. Haley truly paved the way for Americans to discover their own "roots."

There were two more TV series based on Haley's book. *Roots: The Next Generation* appeared in 1979. It starred such great actors as **Ossie Davis** and **Ruby Dee.** *Roots: The Gift* aired in 1988. It continued the story of the Kinte clan. Another Haley book also dealt with African-American history. *A Different Kind of Christmas* told a story of the **UNDERGROUND RAILROAD.** Haley wrote a book about his father's ancestry, called *Queen*. It became a TV mini-series in 1993. It starred a new actress named **Halle Berry.**

A POPULAR SPEAKER: Haley became a favorite speaker all over the country. He enjoyed talking to groups, but it didn't leave much time for writing. When he did need to write, Haley would book passage on a freighter. "At sea, I will work from 10 at night until

Statue of Haley, with his son, William Haley, at the dedication of the Kunta Kinte-Alex Haley Memorial, June 12, 2002.

daybreak," he said. It was a welcome break from the hustle and bustle of his life as a popular speaker.

While on a tour in Seattle in 1992, Haley had a heart attack. He died in Seattle on February 10, 1992. He was celebrated all over the country as a gifted writer and speaker.

ALEX HALEY'S HOME AND FAMILY: Haley married three times. His first wife was named Nannie Branch. They had two children, Lydia and William. After their divorce in 1964, Haley married Juliette Collins. They had one daughter, Cynthia. They divorced in 1972. In 1974, Haley married Myra Lewis.

HIS LEGACY: Alex Haley will always be associated with his famous title *Roots*. It is a word that means much to African-Americans, and to other groups, too. His tale of his family's triumph over the evils of slavery and their achievements inspired generations of Americans.

Haley is also remembered as an advocate for literacy for adults and children. He funded a college scholarship that supports eight students each year from freshman year through graduate school.

The Coast Guard honored one of its most famous sailors by commissioning a boat, the Alex Haley for him. It bears his personal motto: "Find the Good and Praise It."

WORLD WIDE WEB SITES:

http://www.kintehaley.org/
http://www.tnstate.edu/library/digital/Haley.htm
http://www.uscg.mil/pacarea/haley

Virginia Hamilton

1936 - 2002

African-American Author of Books for Children and Young Adults

Creator of *The People Could Fly* and *Her Stories*

VIRGINIA HAMILTON WAS BORN on March 12, 1936, in Yellow Springs, Ohio. Her parents were Kenneth and Etta Hamilton. Kenneth was a farmer and musician. Etta was a homemaker. Virginia was the youngest of five children.

Virginia was very close to her parents. "My dad was the sun around which my world revolved," she said. "My mom, with her quiet, determined way, was my universe."

VIRGINIA HAMILTON GREW UP in a loving family that loved to tell stories. "I come from a long line of storytellers," she recalled. "We didn't simply state facts in our family. Events became happenings. There was always a beginning, a middle, and an end to what we said."

Many of these stories were about her own ancestors. One of her grandfathers had been a slave. His mother helped him escape through the **UNDERGROUND RAILROAD.**

The Underground Railroad was created in the 1850s by people who hated **SLAVERY**. It was a secret system for hiding and moving slaves from the South to the North, and to freedom. After he escaped, Hamilton's grandfather settled in Yellow Springs, Ohio. His story, and others like it, gave her ideas for some of her later writings.

Many members of Hamilton's family lived around Yellow Springs. She grew up visiting relatives and playing with cousins. She also loved exploring the farm country around her.

Hamilton grew up during the Great Depression. That was time in the 1930s when many people were out of work. Some people were hungry. Hamilton's family lived on a farm, so they always had food. But she remembered those who were not as fortunate.

"A strong childhood memory is of the men who passed through our town during the Depression. Men completely broke, many for years without jobs, men who were hungry. 'Do you have work?' they would ask. My father would always find something for them to do. He would leave food by the side of the road for those passing by."

VIRGINIA HAMILTON WENT TO SCHOOL at a small school near her home. She remembered being "the only black girl in my class until 7th grade or so." She always did well in school. She recalled being "teacher's pet." Her teachers gave her lots of "warmth and discipline."

Hamilton also remembered wanting to be a writer. When she was 10, she told her older sister she was going to be famous one day. Hamilton graduated from high school with honors, then went on to college. She attended Antioch College, then Ohio State University.

DECIDING TO BECOME A WRITER: In college, Hamilton studied English. She was still determined to make her living as a writer. Encouraged by a professor, she left college before graduating and moved to New York City. She loved the excitement of big city life. She worked in the mornings as an accountant, then spent her afternoons writing.

She sometimes went out in the evening. She sang with bands, and she met other writers. Sometimes, she stayed home and read. "I read everything I could get my hands on," she recalled.

STARTING TO WRITE FOR CHILDREN: Hamilton says she "never really decided to write for children." She started out writing for adults, then got a call from a college friend who worked in publishing. The friend remembered a story Hamilton had written in college. She encouraged Hamilton to rewrite it as a children's book.

Hamilton did, and the result was *Zeely,* published in 1967. It was a great success with young readers. Hamilton followed it up with more than 30 books for readers of all ages. Some of her books are for beginning readers, some are for middle grade readers, and some are for young adults.

Among her most beloved books for older readers are *The House of Dies Drear* and *The Planet of Junior Brown.* They are mysteries, and give young adults a good scare. Other favorites include *M.C. Higgins the Great.* It won the Newbery Medal in 1975. That's the most important award in children's literature. Three other books, *The Planet of Junior Brown; Sweet Whispers, Brother Rush;* and *In The Beginning: Creation Stories from Around the World,* won Newbery Honors.

Virginia Hamilton became the famous author she knew she'd be when she was 10. Children all over the world read and love her books, which have been translated into many languages.

Hamilton tells stories with African-American children as the main characters. She was one of the first authors to do that. She inspired others to write stories with African-American characters and themes, too. Young readers know her best for her folktales, featured in books like *The People Could Fly* and *Her Stories.*

THE PEOPLE COULD FLY: *The People Could Fly* is based on tales of African-American slaves. Slaves used folktales to pass on their

knowledge and heritage. The tales are funny, and sad.

Hamilton said they were a way for slaves to "express their fears and hopes to one another." Some are simple tales of animals who act like people. Some feature African-American characters.

Some tell of slavery itself. In the title story, "The People Could Fly," slaves are able to fly away from their cruel master. As if by magic, the old slave Toby murmurs the words that set them free.

HER STORIES: Another favorite collection of folktales is *Her Stories*. In that book, Hamilton features stories with African-American heroines. Some of the characters are young and some are old. Hamilton draws her stories from fantasy, legends, and real lives. Together, they form a portrait of African-American life.

JAGUARUNDI: *Jaguarundi*, another book for beginning readers, is set in the rainforest and features animal characters. The main character is the fierce and beautiful jaguarundi, a wild cat. Its home, the rainforest, is threatened by man. Jaguarundi and the other animals must decide whether to leave their forest home. Like slaves, they must escape to freedom. "The story parallels humans who escape their homelands in search of better, safer lives," said Hamilton.

VIRGINIA HAMILTON'S HOME AND FAMILY: Hamilton met her future husband, Arnold Adoff, in New York. Arnold is a writer, poet, and teacher. They married in 1960. Their two children, Leigh and Jaime, are grown up now. They are both musicians.

Hamilton and Adoff moved back to her family's Ohio farm in 1969. They lived in a house on her family's property. "Here on the land is the best place for me to write," she said. "I love the old trees. Being an Ohioan means that I have a long kinship with so many people here, with the landscape and the Ohio sky. For me, there is nothing quite like an Ohio sunset."

Hamilton loved the challenges of being a writer. "I write books because I love chasing after a good story and seeing fantastic characters rising out of the mist of my imaginings. I can't explain how it is I keep having new ideas. But from one book inevitably flows another. It is my way of exploring the known, the remembered, and the imagined, the literary triad of which all stories are made."

Hamilton loved writing for young people, too. "I adore children. For more than 30 years, writing for them has been my pleasure."

Sadly, Virginia Hamilton died of cancer in February 2002. She was 65 years old. Up until her death, Hamilton continued to create books for young readers. Among her last books were *Bluish: A Novel* and *The Girl Who Spun Gold.*

HER LEGACY: Hamilton is remembered as a beloved author for readers of all ages, but especially for the young. "I write for young people because they are our treasure," she once said.

WORLD WIDE WEB SITES:

http://www.eduplace.com/kids/hmr/mtai/hamilton.html
http://www.virginiahamilton.com

Lorraine Hansberry

1930 - 1965

African-American Playwright

Author of *A Raisin in the Sun*

LORRAINE HANSBERRY WAS BORN on May 19, 1930, in Chicago, Illinois. Her parents were Carl and Nannie Hansberry. Together, they owned a successful real estate business. Lorraine was the youngest of four children. Her older siblings were named Mamie, Perry, and Carl.

LORRAINE HANSBERRY GREW UP in a well-to-do, loving family that was committed to equal rights for African-Americans. Both of her parents were descendants of slaves. One of her uncles was a historian of African history.

The family's friends included some of the leading African-American artists and thinkers of the day. **Langston Hughes, Duke Ellington,** and **Paul Robeson** visited the Hansberry home.

Lorraine's parents wanted to do all they could to end discrimination. At that time, all housing in Chicago was separated by race. It was the time of **JIM CROW**, when legal segregation forbade blacks from living where they wished. Carl Hansberry decided to buy a home in the all-white neighborhood of Hyde Park. Right after moving in, the family faced racially motivated attacks.

Lorraine and her sister were sitting in the living room when a brick was thrown through a window. It just missed hitting her. The family received death threats, and faced a lawsuit that forced them to move out. The Hansberrys fought the action in court, and won. But Carl Hansberry was all but broken by the ordeal.

LORRAINE HANSBERRY WENT TO SCHOOL at the local segregated public schools. Her parents could have afforded to send her to private school. But they wanted their children to grow up with other African-Americans.

Lorraine went to Betsy Ross Elementary. She recalled that it was "a ghetto school." Its purpose, she said, was "not to give education, but to withhold as much as possible." It existed "just as the ghetto itself exists not to give people homes, but to cheat them out of as much decent housing as possible."

For high school, Hansberry attended Englewood High. It was a mostly white high school. She had teachers that really challenged her, and she achieved great success.

But Hansberry's life took a tragic turn. In 1946, tired of the persistent racism of the U.S., her father bought a house in Mexico for his family. He was getting ready for them to join him when he died of a stroke.

Lorraine wrote a letter to the *New York Times* about her father. She was convinced that it was racism that had killed him. She outlined what he had sacrificed. "The cost, in emotional turmoil, time, and money led to my father's death."

Around this time, Lorraine developed a keen interest in African history. She studied and learned all she could about Africa, and her own African heritage.

Lorraine graduated from high school in 1948. She went on to college at the University of Wisconsin. The school was then overwhelmingly white. She was the first African-American to live in her dorm. Hansberry didn't find college that challenging. She faced racism, too. She got a "D" in a theater class. The professor, a white male, wanted to discourage her, a black female, from trying to make it in a "white" profession.

Hansberry had had enough of college. She moved to New York. There, she explored her African-American background and developed her writing skills.

LIFE IN NEW YORK: Hansberry loved living in New York. She enjoyed meeting and learning from all kinds of people. She was part of a group of young African-Americans devoted to the struggle for **CIVIL RIGHTS.**

Hansberry got a job with **Paul Robeson** on his magazine *Freedom*. She took an African history course with noted intellectual

Hansberry receives the New York Drama Critics' Circle Award for A Raisin in the Sun, *May 4, 1959.*

W.E.B. Du Bois. (You can read a profile of Du Bois in *Biography for Beginners: African-American Leaders, Volume 1.*)

STARTING TO WRITE: Hansberry was writing her own work, too. To make ends meet, she worked several different jobs, writing in her spare time. She married a student named Robert Nemiroff, who was also a composer. When he sold a song for a lot of money, Hansberry was able to devote herself to writing full-time.

A RAISIN IN THE SUN: Hansberry began to work on what would become her masterpiece, *A Raisin in the Sun*. The title comes from

Langston Hughes's famous poem, "Harlem": "What happens to a dream deferred? Does it dry up, Like a raisin in the sun?"

The play takes place in Chicago. The main characters are the Younger family. They live in a poor, all-black section of Chicago. Their apartment is old and run-down. The father has recently died, and left the family $10,000. Mrs. Younger wants to use the money to buy a house in a white neighborhood. Beneatha, her daughter, wants to use the money to go to medical school. Walter, her son, wants to use the money to start his own business.

They compromise, and Mrs. Younger puts a down payment on a house with one third. She gives the rest to Walter and Beneatha. But Walter loses the money, and with it, the end of their dreams for a better life.

A Raisin in the Sun opened on March 1, 1959, on Broadway. It was a tremendous hit, which surprised everybody, including Hansberry. It was the first play on Broadway with an all-black cast and director. It was also the first to portray African-American life. The play's original cast included such great actors as **Sidney Poitier** and **Ruby Dee.** They went on to star in the successful film version of the play. Hansberry also wrote the screenplay for the film version.

The play won Hansberry the New York Drama Critics' Circle Award. She was the first black dramatist, the youngest dramatist, and only the fifth woman to win the honor. It was a critical moment in the history of drama. **James Baldwin** spoke for many when he noted its importance. "Never before in the history of American theater had so much of the truth of black people's lives been seen on stage."

Hansberry continued to write plays, but nothing ever had the impact of *A Raisin in the Sun.* She wrote a play about slavery and its impact for NBC. But the network thought the topic was "too controversial" and never produced it.

Hansberry also wrote a play called *The Sign in Sidney Brustein's Window.* In subject and tone, it was totally unlike her earlier work. It is about a Jewish man who becomes involved in politics. A play of ideas, it was not what people expected. It didn't please critics or audiences.

Film version of A Raisin in the Sun, *with Sidney Poitier and Ruby Dee.*

A TRAGIC ILLNESS: By the time her second play came out, Hansberry was seriously ill. Tests revealed that she had cancer. She struggled with surgery and chemotherapy, but the illness raged. She fought bravely, but died of cancer on January 12, 1965. She was 34 years old.

LORRAINE HANSBERRY'S HOME AND FAMILY: Hansberry married Robert Nemiroff in 1953. They were close friends, but the marriage did not last. They divorced in 1964, but kept that information a secret. After Hansberry's death, Nemiroff completed her final play, *The Whites.* He also collected her other writings and published them.

HER LEGACY: *A Raisin in the Sun* is considered a major drama of the mid-20th century. Hansberry was the first playwright to bring the true African-American experience to audiences everywhere. The play has been translated into more than 30 languages, and is still produced all over the world.

Before her death, Hansberry spoke to a group of young writers who had won a contest hosted by the United Negro College Fund. In her speech, she told them that "to be young, gifted, and black" was a gift they shouldn't waste. The phrase became famous. Her ex-husband used it as a title for a collection of her work. The phrase inspired Hansberry's friend Nina Simone to write a famous song. Hansberry lives on in her art, inspiring people of all ages.

WORLD WIDE WEB SITES:

http://voices.cla.umn.edu/vg/Bios/entries/hansberry_larraine.html#bio
http://www.kirjasto.sci.fi/corhans.htm
http://www.scils.rutgers.edu/~cybers/hansberry2.html

Langston Hughes

1902 - 1967

African-American Poet, Short Story Writer, and Playwright

Leading Figure of the Harlem Renaissance

LANGSTON HUGHES WAS BORN on February 1, 1902, in Joplin, Missouri. His parents were James and Carrie Hughes. They were both bookkeepers. His parents separated when he was very young.

LANGSTON HUGHES GREW UP in several different places. James Hughes moved to Mexico when Langston was an infant. He and his mother went to visit James and arrived just as an earthquake rocked the city. Langston and his mother returned to Kansas. After that, Langston's parents divorced.

Langston's mother needed to find work. She sent Langston to live with his grandmother in Lawrence, Kansas, while she looked for a job.

LEARNING HIS AFRICAN-AMERICAN LEGACY: Those years living with his grandmother were important ones for Langston. He learned about his rich family heritage. He had black and white ancestors. Some had been slaves, and some had been slave owners. He learned the legacies of **SLAVERY** and The Civil War.

Langston's beloved grandmother was the first black woman to attend Oberlin College. His grandfather had been part of the **ABOLITIONIST** movement. He had joined fiery abolitionist John Brown in the raid on Harper's Ferry and had died there.

Langston's grandmother opened his eyes and his heart to African-American history. He learned about the brutality of slavery. He learned about the lives and hopes of working people. His grandmother took him to hear educator Booker T. Washington. Years later, Hughes would write a poem about Washington and his path from slavery to achievement. (You can read a profile of Washington in *Biography for Beginners: African-American Leaders, Vol. 1.*)

In addition to the stories from his family's past, Langston's life was steeped in the music of the African-American community. The spirituals of the black church, and the blues music of the black community were woven into his daily life. Later, when he became a poet, they would surface again, as themes and rhythms in his verse.

LANGSTON HUGHES WENT TO SCHOOL at the local public schools in Kansas. At school he was seated at the back of the classroom, with the other black students.

When Langston was 12, his grandmother died. His mother, who had remarried, sent for him. So Langston moved to Lincoln, Illinois, to live with his mother and her new husband, Homer Clark.

In Lincoln, Hughes finished elementary school. His fellow students elected him "class poet." The family moved to Cleveland, Ohio. There, Hughes attended Central High School. He did well in school, and was editor of the yearbook.

"THE NEGRO SPEAKS OF RIVERS": Hughes wanted to attend college, but his mother couldn't afford it. He went to visit his father in Mexico. On the train, he wrote one of his first major poems. As he crossed the Mississippi River, the 19-year-old poet thought about the meaning of rivers and black history.

The poem, "The Negro Speaks of Rivers," talks about ancient rivers, like the Nile in Egypt, where black people have lived, and suffered in slavery. It describes the Mississippi, where Abraham Lincoln became convinced that slavery must end. "My soul has grown deep like the rivers," is the last line of this powerful poem. It was published in the **NAACP**'s magazine, *Crisis*, in 1921. Hughes dedicated the poem to the prominent writer and scholar W.E.B. Du Bois. (You can read a profile of Du Bois in *Biography for Beginners: African-American Leaders, Vol. 1.*)

Hughes lived with his father in Mexico for a year. He briefly taught English to the children of wealthy Mexicans. Returning to the U.S., Hughes started college at Columbia University in 1921. His father wanted him to study engineering. But Hughes didn't like his classes. He left Columbia after one year. He wanted to see the world.

TRAVELING THE WORLD: In 1923, Hughes joined the crew of a boat bound for Africa. He worked as a ship's cook. Once they arrived, he traveled through Africa and Europe, working as a dishwasher to pay his expenses. He wrote stories and poems and sent them home to be published. He returned to the U.S. in 1924.

Hughes published his first poetry collection, *The Weary Blues*, in 1926. The title poem describes a weary black piano player. With "his ebony hands on each ivory key," the man plays the "Sweet Blues, Coming from a black man's soul."

Hughes returned to college in 1926. He spent the next three years at Lincoln University in Pennsylvania. That was one of the first all-black colleges in the U.S. While taking classes, Hughes continued to write and publish poems and prose. An important influence on this early work was the poetry of **Paul Laurence Dunbar**. He also spent all the time he could in New York, absorbing the atmosphere of Harlem. He published his first novel, *Not Without Laughter*, in 1929.

When he graduated from Lincoln, Hughes wanted to get a job in publishing and use his writing talents. By that time, he was a published poet and novelist. But doors open to white people were closed to him. Hughes decided to move back to New York and make a living as a writer on his own terms.

THE HARLEM RENAISSANCE: Hughes was part of a group of African-American artists who formed the Harlem Renaissance. The group was based in the Harlem section of New York City. In their poetry, prose, plays, and art work, they celebrated the African-American experience. They used different styles and methods in their works, but shared a common goal. They wanted to create art by black Americans that showcased their talents and dreams.

TRAVELING AND SPEAKING: Hughes visited the noted educator Mary McLeod Bethune at her college in Florida. (You can read a profile of Bethune in *Biography for Beginners: African-American Leaders, Vol. 1.*) She encouraged him to tour the South and hold poetry readings. He did, and audiences loved his work.

Hughes next traveled to the Soviet Union with several other African-Americans. He found much to praise in the country, which seemed to him free of the racism in America.

WRITING PLAYS, POEMS, AND STORIES: Back in the U.S., Hughes continued to write poems, as well as short stories and plays. His subjects were the people, places, and ways of life that he knew. He founded a theater group, the Harlem Suitcase Theater. His plays ran on the weekends, and admission was just 35 cents. They were written for working black people, who loved them. He founded similar theaters in Los Angeles and Chicago.

Yet some members of the black community didn't like Hughes's work. He tried hard to duplicate the language of simple folk. Some people objected to that. They thought he should feature educated blacks who'd achieved success. But that wasn't for Hughes. "I felt that the masses of our people had as much in their lives to put into books as did those more fortunate ones," he said. He wanted to show the lives of "the people I had grown up with."

Pen and ink drawing of Hughes by Winold Reiss, 1927.

Hughes championed other African-American artists, too. William Grant Still was an African-American composer. He was the first black to have a symphony he wrote performed by a major orchestra. Hughes wrote the words for an opera Still composed, *Troubled Island*. It opened in New York in 1949. In the 1950s, he wrote poems to be read to jazz music. He recorded some of these with music contributed by jazz musician Charles Mingus.

JESSE B. SIMPLE: Hughes wrote a series of columns for the *Chicago Defender* about a character named "Jesse B. Simple." Simple became one of Hughes's most famous creations. He is a storyteller who lives in Harlem. He tells his stories of African-American life to a writer named Boyd. Simple is funny, warm, and open. He became the main character in a book of Hughes's short stories, *Simple Speaks His Mind.* Simple reappeared in two more short story collections and a play.

BOOKS FOR YOUNG READERS: Hughes also wrote books for young readers. Most of them were histories and biographies of famous African-Americans. He wrote collections of poems for young readers, too. *The Dream Keeper and Other Poems* is one of these collections. His poems are still read, studied, and enjoyed today by young people all over the world.

"HARLEM: WHAT HAPPENS TO A DREAM DEFERRED?" One of Hughes's most famous poems is called "Harlem," published in 1942. It is also known by its famous first line: "What happens to a dream deferred?" In the poem, Hughes talks about the dreams and hopes of African-Americans. When a dream is "deferred"—made to wait—what happens then?

> What happens to a dream deferred?
> Does it dry up
> Like a raisin in the sun?

The last lines are dark and threatening:

> Maybe it just sags
> Like a heavy load.
>
> *Or does it explode?*

The poem shares the themes and simple language of much of Hughes's poetry. Its powerful message tells of the seething frustration of people denied their right to hope for a better future.

Lorraine Hansberry used a line from this famous poem as the title of her famous play, *A Raisin in the Sun.*

In the 1950s, anti-Communist fervor gripped the country. People like **Paul Robeson** and W.E.B. Du Bois were condemned for their pro-Communist leanings. Because he had spoken positively of the Communist Soviet Union in the 1930s, Hughes also was condemned. He defended himself by saying he no longer held the same opinions of the Soviet Union. Some activists found his new stance unbelievable. They thought he was saying whatever he had to, to protect himself. In the eyes of some African-Americans, his reputation fell.

Hughes continued to write poems, stories, essays, and plays until his death in 1967. As he grew older, the fight for **CIVIL RIGHTS** grew more militant. In the 1960s, some African-American activists accused him of being uncommited to the cause. Yet he remained steadfast in his strong pride as an African-American. He refused to let rage at racism overcome him. Instead, he continued to celebrate African-American life as he knew it. He felt he could condemn injustice in poetry that could remain positive about the hope for equality for all.

LANGSTON HUGHES'S HOME AND FAMILY: Hughes spent most of his adult life living in Harlem, on East 127th Street. He never married or had children. He died of cancer on May 22, 1967, in New York. His home is now a landmark, and East 127th Street is now Langston Hughes Place.

HIS LEGACY: Langston Hughes is considered one of the finest poets of the 20th century. His poetry contributed to the flowering of the Harlem Renaissance. His simple, musical verse contained deep, important themes. His poetry celebrated African-American life and condemned the racism and injustice that would limit that life. His deeply affecting poetry featured the lives of the "low-down folks" he knew so well. He celebrated them in verses full of the rhythm of blues and jazz, in poetry that continues to inspire new generations.

WORLD WIDE WEB SITES:

http://www.americaslibrary.gov.cgi-bin/page.cgi/aa/writers/hughes
http://www.poets.org/poet.php/prmPID/83

Zora Neale Hurston

1891? - 1960

African-American Anthropologist, Dramatist, Essayist, and Autobiographer

ZORA NEALE HURSTON WAS BORN around January 7, 1891, in Notasulga, Alabama. At different times in her life, Hurston claimed to have been born in several different places, and in different years. She often claimed to have been born in Eatonville, Florida, where she grew up. A family Bible indicated she was born in Alabama, in 1891.

Her parents were John and Lucy Ann Hurston. John was a minister in the Baptist church. Lucy Ann was a former teacher who stayed home to raise her eight children. Zora was the fifth child.

She had six brothers: Hezekiah, John, Richard, Clifford, Benjamin, and Everett. She had one sister, Sarah.

ZORA NEALE HURSTON GREW UP in the township of Eatonville, Florida. It was a remarkable place. It was the first incorporated black township in the country. That means it was the first self-governing African-American community in the U.S. The citizens of Eatonville were justly proud of their town. Reverend John Hurston served as mayor of the township for years.

Zora loved growing up in Eatonville. The atmosphere of independent, hard-working African-Americans influenced her all her life. She also loved to listen to the townspeople tell stories. Later on, when she became a writer, she used her memories of those times and those stories.

Zora was a lively child. Her mother, especially, encouraged her energy and spirit. She told all her children they should "jump at the sun." She thought they could be anything they wanted to be. She wanted them to use all their unique gifts to make a difference in the world.

EARLY SCHOOLING: Zora went to Hungerford Elementary in Eatonville. Thanks to her mother, she learned to read before she went to school. She loved reading, and it showed. One day, a group of white women visiting her school heard Zora read. They were so impressed that they bought her a gift—a huge box of books.

A FAMILY TRAGEDY: In 1904, Zora and her family faced a terrible tragedy. Her beloved mother died, and the family was in crisis. Her father couldn't care for all the children. He sent them to live with relatives.

Zora was sent to live in Jacksonville, Florida. It was her first experience of racism. Those were the days of **JIM CROW**. Facilities, from schools to restaurants to buses, were legally segregated by race. It was a shock."Jacksonville made me know that I was a little colored girl," Hurston remembered. She liked her school, though, and she did well.

STRUGGLING TO SURVIVE: When her father remarried, things got even worse for the Hurston children. Her new stepmother didn't want Zora or her siblings around. They were still living with relatives, but her father stopped sending money for their living expenses.

The Hurston children were uprooted again. They were sent off to live with other relatives. Hurston remembered feeling like she was "being passed around like a bad penny." Just a teenager, Zora had to find jobs as a maid just to live. It was a terrible time. "I wanted family love and peace and a resting place," she wrote later. "I wanted books and school."

Hurston got a job as a maid with an opera troupe that performed Gilbert and Sullivan. She traveled all over the country with them. After a few years, she decided to go back to school.

BACK TO SCHOOL: In 1917, at the age of 26, Hurston returned to school. She went to the Morgan Academy in Baltimore, Maryland. She did well, and after graduating in 1918, went on to college.

COLLEGE: Hurston went to Howard University in Washington, D.C. That's one of the best traditional black colleges in the country. She had to work several jobs to pay for school, and after five years had only two-years worth of credits. But she loved to learn.

Hurston also wrote stories that were published in the school magazine. The editor was impressed with her ability. He encouraged her to go to New York.

MOVING TO NEW YORK—THE HARLEM RENAISSANCE: Hurston moved to New York in 1924. It was the time of the Harlem Renaissance. That was a period, from the 1920s through the 1930s, when many African-American artists moved to New York. Many lived in the section of the city called Harlem. Writers like Hurston and **Langston Hughes**, musicians like **Duke Ellington** and artsts like **Romare Bearden** created some of their best work at that time. Many of their creations were based on themes of African-American life. It was the first time that many artists had turned to their African-American roots for inspiration.

Hurston became part of the writing world of Harlem. She wrote award-winning plays and stories. She decided she had even more to learn, so she returned to college.

MORE COLLEGE: Hurston became a student at Barnard College. When Hurston attended, it was an all-girls school. And she was the only African-American student.

Hurston studied anthropology (an-throw-POL-ah-gee). That is the study of cultures—the way that people live. Her professor was the famous Frank Boas. He taught her to recognize that the stories and songs of her youth were part of the anthropology of African-Americans. She had found what she really wanted to study.

TRAVELING IN THE SOUTH: In 1927, Hurston set out for the Southern states. She traveled for several months, stopping to collect songs and folktales from black communities. These would become

the source of some of her greatest work. Hurston graduated from Barnard in 1928.

LIFE AS A WRITER: After college, Hurston began her career as a full-time writer. She worked on a play with **Langston Hughes**, called *Mule Bone*. But the two had a falling out. She completed the play by herself. When it was produced, she didn't mention his contribution. They were never friends again.

Hurston published several short stories, including one called "The Gilded Six-Bits." It caught the attention of a major publisher. They wanted to publish her work. She wrote a novel for them, *Jonah's Gourd Vine.*

Hurston's next major work was *Mules and Men*, published in 1935. It was based on her folktale collections. It was a controversial work for some African-Americans. Many works of the time by black writers were about racism and the fight for equality. Hurston didn't write about those things. Instead, she wrote about happy, contented lives in African-American communities.

Her critics thought she was ignoring the truth. She disagreed. "I do not belong to the sobbing school of Negrohood," she said. She didn't believe that "nature had given them a lowdown dirty deal."

THEIR EYES WERE WATCHING GOD: In 1937, Hurston published her best-known work, *Their Eyes Were Watching God.* It is a novel about a woman named Janie Crawford and her three marriages. It is a story of love and loss, set in Florida, the land she knew so well.

A SCANDAL: In her later years, Hurston's life was nearly ruined by a scandal. She was falsely accused of molesting a child. The accusation was proved false, and she was never charged. But the scandal hurt her reputation.

LATER YEARS: Wounded by the scandal, Hurston moved to Florida. She had made very little money from her writing. To make ends meet, she wrote articles and worked as a maid. She had a stroke in 1959. Hurston died in Fort Pierce, Florida, on January 28, 1960.

This formerly famous author died alone and poor. But over the years her work has been rediscovered and celebrated. In 2005, **Oprah Winfrey** produced a television version of *Their Eyes Were Watching God*. It starred **Halle Berry** in the title role. Through the efforts of Winfrey and others, a new generation of readers is discovering Hurston's work.

WORKS FOR YOUNG READERS: Several years ago, some of Hurston's folktales were adapted for young readers. They are illustrated by such great artists as Faith Ringgold and Christopher Myers.

ZORA NEALE HURSTON'S HOME AND FAMILY: Hurston was married twice. She and her first husband, Howard Sheen, were married from 1927 to 1931. Several years later, she married a man named Albert Price. Their marriage lasted from 1939 to 1943. She did not have children.

HER LEGACY: Hurston is remembered for colorful recreations of African-American life. In works like *Their Eyes Were Watching God*, she showed her love of the black communities and culture of the South. Her work is read and enjoyed today as an example of the flowering of African-American literature in the 20th century.

WORLD WIDE WEB SITES:

http://www.lkwdpl.org/wihohio/hurs-zorx.htm
http://www.zoranealehurston.com/

Judith Jamison

1944 -

African-American Dancer and Choreographer
Director of the Alvin Ailey American Dance Theater

JUDITH JAMISON WAS BORN on May 10, 1944, In Philadelphia, Pennsylvania. (Her last name is pronounced "JAM-is-in.") Her parents were Tessie and John Jamison. Tessie was a teacher and John was a sheet-metal worker. Both her parents were fine musicians. Her father once planned on a career as a professional piano player. But after starting a family, he chose instead to be laborer for the steady income it provided. Judith has one older brother, John.

JUDITH JAMISON GREW UP in the Germantown section of Philadelphia. Her grandparents lived next door. She had a wonderful childhood, full of music and family love. Her parents enjoyed all kinds of music, from classical to gospel.

Judith grew up loving music, too. She studied piano with her dad. His love for family, and for music, was a great influence on her. She remembers him playing "with a complete release of passion." She recalled how he would play music with such warmth, "then work from nine to five with drills and nails and hammers."

Judith studied piano, violin, and sang in the church choir. The family attended the Mother Bethel African Methodist Episcopal Church. It is the oldest black church in the country. There, Judith fell in love with the music and rituals of worship. "I saw what the spirit could do," she recalled. "And how it could change your life."

She was always in motion as a child. "I thought I wanted to be a pilot or drive something that had a powerful engine. A train or a plane or an aircraft carrier. I have always been one of those people who know exactly what they want."

STARTING TO DANCE: In dance, Judith found expression for all that she loved: music, movement, and spirit. She started taking ballet lessons at the age of six. She loved it. She took all kinds of dance from that point on. In addition to ballet, she studied tap, jazz, and acrobatics.

Judith loved to perform. She even remembers her first dance costume. "I wore a red-checkered shirt, blue jeans, and pink ballet shoes," she recalled. "I danced to 'I'm an Old Cowhand'."

JUDITH JAMISON WENT TO SCHOOL at the local public schools in Philadelphia. She was always an excellent student. She gradu-

Portrait of Jamison from May 1979.

ated from high school one year early, and went on to Fisk University. That's an outstanding traditional black college in Nashville, Tennessee. After three semesters of college, Jamison had made up her mind. She wanted a career in dance.

Jamison returned to Philadelphia and studied dance full-time. She took classes at the Philadelphia Dance Academy. She had studied ballet for years. Now, for the first time, she studied modern dance.

MODERN DANCE: Modern dance is different from traditional ballet in several ways. Ballet movements stress length and height. Modern dance is rooted in the ground. Jamison describes it like this: “Classical dance is usually danced very high in space, on pointe. Modern dancers are very much into the floor.” Modern dances often include deep bends, angular movements, and broad, sweeping turns.

In 1964, Jamison took a dance class with Agnes De Mille. De Mille was a famous modern dance choreographer. She created the original dances in Broadway musicals like *Oklahoma!* De Mille thought Jamison had the potential to be a star.

STARTING TO DANCE IN NEW YORK: De Mille invited Jamison to perform in New York City in her new ballet, *The Four Marys*. Jamison made her New York debut in December 1964, dancing in the role with the American Ballet Theater.

After her debut, she had trouble finding additional roles to dance. She went to many auditions, but didn’t get jobs. She thought there were two reasons. One, at 5′ 10″, she was very tall for a ballerina. And at that time, there were no African-American dancers in major dance companies.

Jamison was determined to make her life in dance. While auditioning for a TV special, she was spotted by **Alvin Ailey.** He was an up-and-coming black choreographer. He asked Jamison to audition for him. She did, and thought she’d done a terrible job. But three days later, he called and asked her to join his company. She did. It was a decision that would determine her life’s work.

JOINING THE ALVIN AILEY AMERICAN DANCE THEATER: Alvin Ailey was one of the first major black choreographers. His dances, often set to black spirituals, celebrated the African-American experience. They showed his love and knowledge of ballet, Broadway, jazz, and modern dance.

Jamison started dancing with Ailey in 1965. She was one of his greatest dancers, and his inspiration. She was tall, powerful, and dynamic. When she joined Ailey, there were only 10 dancers in the company. They were young, talented, and often broke.

Jamison with dancer Renee Robinson, in the wings at the official opening of the Joan Weill Center for Dance, March 1, 2005.

Jamison danced with the company for 15 years. Often, the company had to disband because they ran out of money. At those points, Jamison joined other companies and danced all over the world.

One of Jamison's most famous roles is Ailey's *Revelations*. It is a series of dances set to spirituals. She showed her great technique and power, but also her heart.

Another famous dance Ailey created just for her is called *Cry*. He dedicated it to "all black women, especially our mothers." Jamison remembers its creation. "*Cry* was created in eight days," she recalled. "We barely said anything to each other." That was how closely they understood each other.

The Ailey troupe toured the world. Their visit to Africa had a powerful effect on Jamison. "The diversity and beauty of the continent hit me in the face, the spirit, and the heart," she recalled. "I very much wanted to be identified as being from somewhere on the continent. In Senegal, I was told that I looked like a member of the Peul tribe. My coloring was very much like theirs, as were my facial features. I was tickled when I learned that the Peul were nomadic. They were gypsies; so was I."

BROADWAY: Jamison decided to leave the Ailey company in 1980 to perform in a Broadway musical. She sang and danced in the hit show *Sophisticated Ladies*. It was based on the music of the legendary **Duke Ellington**.

After two years on Broadway, Jamison was ready for a rest. She took two years off from performing and lived in her home in rural Connecticut. She enjoyed the time off, but soon was ready to work again. "Once you're given the gift, you just can't go off into the sunset," she said.

BECOMING A CHOREOGRAPHER: Jamison started to create her own dances. Her first dance, *Divining*, debuted in 1984, with the Ailey company. It was a great success. Since then, she's choreographed many of the company's most beloved works. These include *Rift, Riverside, Sweet Release,* and *Hymn*.

THE JAMISON PROJECT: In 1988, Jamison formed her own company. Called the Jamison Project, the group performed all over the country for a few years. Then, Jamison received some tragic news. Her mentor and friend, Alvin Ailey, had died. Two weeks after his death, in December 1989, Jamison took over the Ailey company.

BECOMING ARTISTIC DIRECTOR OF THE AILEY COMPANY: Jamison revealed that she and Ailey had talked about her taking over, years earlier. "I knew it was what I had to do," she recalled.

Six-year-old students attending the Ailey company's First Step program, March 1, 2005.

"Alvin nurtured me, took care of me, and gave me so much. Now, he's given me this great gift. And I'm going to take care of it."

Jamison has been the artistic director of the Ailey company for 18 years now. She says it's like being a "salesperson, nurse, mother, psychoanalyst, and rehearsal director." She honors Ailey's memory by continuing to showcase his many wonderful dances. She still choreographs, too, but also encourages new talent. "I don't feel I'm standing in anyone's shoes. I'm standing on Alvin's shoulders. The horizons become broader."

Like Ailey, Jamison is committed to outreach programs that bring dance and the arts to the African-American community. She wants to reach out to "young audiences that are not used to concert dance." She especially wants them to understand that "concert dance is a reflection of themselves, a part of their lives."

As the artistic director, she also heads the dance school. She helps develop and train young dancers, and get them ready to join dance companies. She's still creating dances, including one performed at the 1996 Olympics. And in 2002, she carried the Olympic torch herself, in Salt Lake City. In 2005, she oversaw the development of a permanent home for the Ailey company in New York City. In February 2008, Jamison announced that she would retire as director of the Ailey company in 2011. As the search for her successor begins, Jamison says she will remain a part of the company she helped to build for a long time to come.

JUDITH JAMISON'S HOME AND FAMILY: Jamison lives in New York City. She was briefly married in the 1970s to another Ailey dancer, Miguel Godreau. They are now divorced.

Jamison has always loved to cook. She says that if she could invite three people in all of history to dinner, they would be "Nelson Mandela, Maya Angelou, and Alvin Ailey."

HER LEGACY: Judith Jamison is one of the most important figures in modern dance. As a dancer, her abilities inspired some of Alvin Ailey's greatest choreography. As director of the Ailey company, she has preserved and nurtured the dances of her mentor, as she has developed new talent and inspired a generation of dancers. She is a woman of great gifts, which she shares abundantly with the world.

WORLD WIDE WEB SITES:

http://www.alvinailey.org/
http://www.kennedy-center.org/calendar/

Jacob Lawrence
1917 - 2000
African-American Artist

JACOB LAWRENCE WAS BORN on September 7, 1917, in Atlantic City, New Jersey. His full name was Jacob Armstead Lawrence. His parents were Jacob and Rosalee Lawrence. They had moved to the North from the South as part of a great migration of African-Americans in the early 1900s. They were looking for better jobs in the North. They wanted better opportunities for themselves and their children. Jacob was the oldest of three children, with a brother, William, and a sister, Geraldine.

JACOB LAWRENCE GREW UP in several different places. The family moved to Easton, Pennsylvania, when Jacob was two. His father worked in the mines for several years, then lost his job. He found a job as a railroad cook, but the money and work worries made life difficult.

Jacob's parents separated when he was seven. His mother moved the family to Philadelphia. There, she found work as a domestic servant. Jacob remembered taking care of his brother and sister while his mother worked.

But his mother wasn't able to make ends meet. When Jacob was 10, she put the children in foster care and moved to Harlem, in New York City. Jacob and his siblings lived in foster care for three years. Then, when he was 13, his mother moved all the children to New York to live with her.

Harlem was a rough and dangerous place then. Jacob didn't feel happy at school or in the neighborhood. His mother was afraid he'd join a gang. She found him a wonderful place for him to spend his free time.

EARLY ART EXPERIENCES: Jacob's mother enrolled him in art workshops at the 135th Street Library. He also took courses at the Utopia Neighborhood Center.

His teacher was Charles Alston, an African-American painter and artist. He encouraged Jacob to explore art in any way he wished. Jacob liked to paint simple shapes, like triangles and squares, in different colors. Then he began to create paper-mache masks.

Jacob also began to create murals, using cut-up cardboard boxes. He'd paint scenes from life on the streets of Harlem. It was the start of what would become his life's work.

JACOB LAWRENCE WENT TO SCHOOL at the local public schools, in Philadelphia and New York. He went to P.S. 89 elementary school in New York, then to Frederick Douglass Junior High. He went on to the New York High School of Commerce. It was a vocational school designed to help students find jobs. Jacob hoped to become a commercial artist. But Jacob was unhappy there. He dropped out after two years.

When Jacob was in high school, the country was suffering through the Great Depression. That was a time in the 1930s when up to 25% of Americans lost their jobs. One of those was Jacob's mother. When she couldn't find work, the family went on welfare. Jacob helped out any way he could. He got a paper route, worked as a delivery boy, and did other odd jobs.

In 1936, Lawrence got a job with the Civilian Conservation Corps (CCC). That was a national program that trained people and helped them find jobs during the Depression.

BECOMING PART OF THE HARLEM ART WORLD: Despite these hardships, Lawrence kept up his art studies. He took classes at the Harlem Art Workshop and the Harlem Community Center. He went to museums and read about African-American history and African art.

Lawrence started to rent studio space from his mentor, Charles Alston, for $8 a month. Through Alston, he met some of the greatest African-American artists of the time. It was the end of the incredible flowering of African-American art known as the **HARLEM RENAISSANCE**. He met the poet **Langston Hughes,** and the novelist **Ralph Ellison**. He also met fellow artists **Romare Bearden** and Gwendolyn Knight. She would become his wife.

Surrounded by these fellow artists, Lawrence began to paint works like *Street Orator* and *Clinic*. These scenes of life in Harlem were featured in the first exhibit of his work, at the Harlem Artists Guild.

Another important artist and mentor was Augusta Savage. She helped Lawrence get backing from the Works Progress Administration (WPA). Like the CCC, the WPA was a national program that supported people during the Depression. Lawrence started receiving $26 a week. It allowed him to paint full-time. He was incredibly grateful to Savage. "If Augusta Savage hadn't insisted on getting me onto the project, I don't think I could ever have become an artist," he recalled.

Lawrence completed enough paintings to exhibit his first one-man show in 1938. His paintings were widely seen, and widely admired. He was on his way.

PAINTING THE AFRICAN-AMERICAN EXPERIENCE: Lawrence's most famous works combined art and history, his two great passions. He did research into African-American history. It fascinated him.

Lawrence's first major work was a series of paintings on the life of Toussaint L'Ouverture (too-SAHN loo-ver-TUER). He was a revolutionary leader who established the island nation of Haiti. Lawrence created a sequence of panels, with brief captions describing his hero's life. He began to develop his signature style: a series of panels full of bright color, arranged to tell a story.

Lawrence had a system when he worked on a series. He laid out the panels on the floor of his studio. He drew sketches, and composed captions. Then he painted the panels, one color at a time. He started with black, then lighter colors. He wanted to make sure the color didn't vary throughout the series.

Next, Lawrence painted panels picturing the lives of Frederick Douglass and Harriet Tubman. He celebrated the lives of these two great **ABOLITIONISTS.** He also painted a series of works on the fiery abolitionist John Brown.

Lawrence became best known for his pictures of African-American life. One of his most important is a 60-panel series called *The Migration Series*. It tells the story of the blacks who moved from the South to the North, in search of work. It was his own family's story, too. Lawrence made it a universal tale, through his art. He repeated images, including a spike and a nail, to show the similar hopes, dreams, struggles, and achievements of African-Americans.

The Migration Series was first shown in New York in 1942. The series then toured the country for two years. During that time, the U.S. entered World War II. Lawrence joined the Coast Guard and served for two years. While in the service, Lawrence painted a series on the lives of soldiers.

After the war, Lawrence continued to paint. He taught at colleges, and developed new techniques. One of the influences on his painting was jazz music. Lawrence conveyed the rhythmic and

tonal changes of jazz in works of vibrant color. He created a series devoted to his memories of performances at Harlem's famed Apollo Theater.

Lawrence also suffered from depression for several years. He went into a hospital for treatment. That treatment, and the constant love and support of his wife, helped him through those difficult times. He resumed painting, and even took his art in new directions.

Lawrence started to illustrate books, and he created books of his own. He wrote a book based on his famous *Migration* series. He wrote what he was trying to accomplish with the work. "Out of the struggle comes a kind of power, and even beauty. I tried to convey this in the rhythm of the pictures, in the repetition of images." He illustrated children's books, too. He created a book based on his series on Harriet Tubman. It's titled *Harriet and the Promised Land.*

JACOB LAWRENCE'S HOME AND FAMILY: Lawrence met his wife, Gwendolyn Knight, when they were young artists in Harlem. They married in 1941. They didn't have any children. Lawrence died on June 9, 2000. He was 82 years old.

HIS LEGACY: Lawrence was the first African-American artist to celebrate the history and culture of black Americans. He is considered one of the most important African-American artists of the 20th century.

WORLD WIDE WEB SITES:

http://www.pbslorg.newhour/bb/remember
http://www.whitney.org/jacoblawrence/

Spike Lee
1957 -
African-American Filmmaker and Actor

SPIKE LEE WAS BORN on March 20, 1957, in Atlanta, Georgia. "Spike" is a nickname. His name when he was born was Shelton Jackson Lee. His parents were Bill and Jacquelyn Lee. Bill is a jazz musician and Jacquelyn was a teacher. Spike has a sister named Joie and brothers named Cinque, Chris, and David.

SPIKE LEE GREW UP in Brooklyn, New York, where his family moved when he was young. He grew up in a loving, nurturing family. His mother gave him the nickname Spike when she saw his determined, tough nature.

Spike's parents taught him to study and admire the works of African-American artists. "I was forced to read **Langston Hughes**," he recalls. "And I'm glad my mother made me do that." His dad encouraged him to listen to the music of jazz trumpeter **Miles Davis**.

All the early exposure to African-American art and history made a deep impression on Lee. It would become the source for his later movies.

SPIKE LEE WENT TO SCHOOL in Brooklyn. His mother taught at a private school, where the students were mostly white. He could have gone there, but Spike chose to go to public school, where his fellow students were black.

After graduating from high school, Lee attended Morehouse College. That is one of the finest traditional black colleges in the country. He started making films at Morehouse, and found out what he wanted to do for the rest of his life. He went on to graduate school at New York University. He produced a film there called *Joe's Bed-Stuy Barbershop: We Cut Heads*. It won a student Academy Award.

STARTING TO MAKE MOVIES: When Lee started out making movies, he had to work during the day for living expenses. He got a job with a film distributor. He shipped movies during the day, and tried to write and raise funds to make films at night. His first attempt was called *The Messenger*. But the money to produce the film never came through. The project had to be abandoned, unfinished.

Next, Lee wrote and filmed a movie called *She's Gotta Have It*. The film cost $175,000 to make. Lee went into debt to finish it. To

Lee as Mookie and Danny Aiello as Sal in Do the Right Thing, *1989.*

his surprise, it was a hit. The movie made $7 million. Its success meant that Lee was able to make the films he wanted to make.

Lee's next film was *School Daze.* Like most of his films, it's about African-American life. And like most of his films, it was controversial. In the movie, Lee examines how African-Americans discriminate against each other based on their skin color. His next movie would be about race, too, but about black-white relations.

DO THE RIGHT THING: Lee made *Do the Right Thing* in 1989. It is a deep, often painful look at race relations. It takes place in Brooklyn, and deals with the tensions between the African-American and Italian-American communities. Lee shows what happens when tensions lead to violence. It made Americans, black and white, confront some hard truths about race in America.

Lee's next film was *Mo' Better Blues.* It featured the famous actor **Denzel Washington**. The two would work together again on one of Lee's best-known films, *Malcolm X.*

MALCOLM X: In *Malcolm X* Lee depicts the life of the fiery **CIVIL RIGHTS** leader Malcolm X. (You can read a profile about him in

Lee as Shorty in Malcolm X, *1992.*

Biography for Beginners: African-American Leaders, Volume 1.) Washington and Lee brought the passionate, controversial leader to life, and to the attention of a new generation. Washington received an Academy Award nomination for his performance.

Lee continued to focus on African-American life in *Crooklyn*, about a middle class family in Brooklyn. In 1997, he produced a documentary called *4 Little Girls*. It tells the tragic and true story of the four girls killed when their church was bombed in Birmingham, Alabama, in 1963.

FEATURING OUTSTANDING PERFORMANCES BY DAVIS AND DEE: Lee has always featured some of the country's finest black actors in his films. Two of them are **Ossie Davis** and **Ruby Dee.** They appeared in several of his movies, including *Do the Right Thing* and *Jungle Fever*. Like Lee, Davis and Dee have devoted themselves to acting, and to the struggle for equality for African-Americans.

Lee in a scene from When the Levees Broke, *2006.*

WHEN THE LEVEES BROKE: One of Lee's most recent films is a documentary about the Hurricane Katrina disaster. It's called *When the Levees Broke*. Lee shows the devastation of New Orleans after the storm, and the delays in government aid to the disaster victims. He was very clear about why he made the film. "It was a very painful experience to see my fellow American citizens, the majority of them African-Americans, in the dire situation they were in. And I was outraged with the slow response of the federal government."

WRITING CHILDREN'S BOOKS: Recently, Lee and his wife, Tonya, have begun writing books for young readers. The first, *Please, Baby, Please*, is about a rambunctious toddler. She's got great energy, and doesn't feel like following directions. In their second book, the Lees change the story a bit. In *Please, Puppy, Please*, two young children try to get their new puppy to behave. Young readers enjoy both books, and their warm, funny message.

FUTURE PLANS: Spike Lee is in the middle of great film career. He plans to make movies for years to come. He's also produced ads, including some famous ones with Michael Jordan.

40 ACRES AND A MULE: Lee's production company is called "40 Acres and a Mule." The name refers to the promise made to freed slaves at the end of the Civil War. They were told by the government that they would receive 40 acres and a mule to begin their lives as freed men and women. The lands they were given were later taken away, and given back to the plantation owners. Lee keeps the memory of promises made, and broken, alive in his company's name.

SPIKE LEE'S HOME AND FAMILY: Lee married Tonya Lewis in 1993. They have two children, a daughter named Satchel and a son named Jackson. They live in New York. Lee's parents and siblings have also been involved in his films. His dad has written music for his movies. His sister and brother have appeared in his films, too.

Lee is a huge fan of the New York Knicks basketball team. He goes to almost all the games, and sits in a courtside seat.

HIS LEGACY: Spike Lee is one of the best-known and most highly respected filmmakers of the era. He creates movies that make people think about race. While he's sometimes controversial, he tries to tell the truth, as he sees it, about America, its problems, and its potential.

WORLD WIDE WEB SITES:

http://efilmcritic.com/feature.php?feature=141
http://www.biography.com/search/article.do?id=9377207
http://www.imbd.com/name/nm0000490/bio

Wynton Marsalis

1961 -

African-American Musician, Bandleader, and Composer

WYNTON MARSALIS WAS BORN on October 18, 1961, in New Orleans, Louisiana. His parents are Ellis and Dolores Marsalis. Ellis taught music for years, and is now a jazz pianist. Dolores, who is now a homemaker, used to be a jazz singer and teacher.

Wynton is the second of six sons in the family. Like their parents, the Marsalis brothers are all very musical. Branford, who is older, is a saxophone player and musical director. Wynton's younger brothers Jason and Delfeayo are also musicians, and Ellis III is a computer consultant. His youngest brother, Mboya, is autistic. Because of his disability, Mboya lives at home with his parents.

GROWING UP AND MAKING MUSIC: Wynton grew up in the town of Kenner, near New Orleans. From a very early age, it was obvious that he had great musical talent. He started playing the trumpet when he was only five. When he was just eight, he was playing jazz in his church marching band.

Marsalis grew up near New Orleans, one of the major centers of jazz music. He loved jazz from the start. He remembers that he learned the music from "a generation of older musicians." These people "loved music so much they would do anything for us."

These older musicians wanted to pass on their knowledge of the music they loved. One of Wynton's first teachers was a man named John Longo. Longo would give Marsalis "two and three-hour lessons, never looking at the clock."

JAZZ AND CLASSICAL MUSIC: Marsalis is one of the most gifted talents in music. He can play jazz and classical music equally well. The two types of music take different talents. Classical music takes practice in playing technical pieces well. Jazz is based on "improvisation." That is actually making up music as a piece is being played. To play jazz, a musician has to understand melodies, harmonies, and the structure of a piece. Jazz musicians make their unique contribution to a piece by composing on the spot.

Marsalis understands and loves to perform both types of music. Even when he was growing up, he could play them both beautifully. Two special influences on his entire career were **Louis Armstrong** and **Duke Ellington.**

WYNTON MARSALIS WENT TO SCHOOL at the local public schools. He went to high school at Benjamin Franklin High School

in New Orleans. He also continued private music lessons. And he took special classes in "music theory"—the study of the structure of a piece.

By the time Marsalis was in high school, he had formed a funk band with his brother. He was also performing in marching bands, jazz bands, and playing with adults in classical orchestras.

Marsalis claims he was a "wild kid" in school, but he had excellent grades. When it came time to decide on college, he chose a school where he could devote himself to music. He went to the Julliard School in New York City. That's one of the finest schools in the country for musicians and artists.

Marsalis spent just two years at Julliard. He enjoyed his studies in classical music, but he was disappointed in the way jazz was treated. He wanted to study jazz seriously. Yet he felt that his teachers didn't treat the music with respect. "When you play jazz

Marsalis at a tribute to Duke Ellington.

at Julliard, people laugh," he said later. So he left college to start his career in music.

MAKING A CAREER IN MUSIC: Marsalis had already played with major jazz groups when he began to play full time in 1981. He had played with such jazz greats as Art Blakey and the Jazz Messengers. Now he started playing with Herbie Hancock's group. They toured and recorded together, and Marsalis learned even more about the jazz music he loved.

In 1982, Marsalis formed his own group. It was a jazz trio that included his brother Branford. They performed and made recordings that became big hits.

But Marsalis never left his love of classical music behind. At the same time that he was touring and playing with his jazz group, he was also performing and recording classical music. In fact, in 1983, two of his recordings, one jazz and one classical, won Grammy awards. He was the first musician ever to win in both categories.

In addition to playing, touring, and composing, Marsalis devotes himself to a major center for jazz at Lincoln Center in New York.

JAZZ AT LINCOLN CENTER: Marsalis has worked as head of Jazz at Lincoln Center in New York for years. He programs concerts, performs, and composes for the series. He's also introduced an important educational program. He hopes to reach kids of all ages and get them interested in jazz.

Bringing the joy and importance of music to young people is very important to Marsalis. He teaches music in schools all over the country. He holds workshops for young players every year.

He's also brought his love of music to television. His series "Marsalis on Music" ran on PBS stations all over the country. He taught viewers of all ages about all different kinds of music. Marsalis was also the main consultant for Ken Burns in his *Jazz* series on PBS.

As a composer, Marsalis has written works for ballet and modern dance companies, and also symphonies. One of his works,

Marsalis performing for school children.

Blood on the Fields, is a jazz "oratorio" about **SLAVERY.** An oratorio is like an opera. It tells a story with words and music. *Blood on the Fields* has been performed all over the world. Marsalis won the Pulitzer Prize for *Blood on the Fields.* He is the first jazz musician to ever win that important award.

HURRICANE KATRINA: In August 2005, Hurricane Katrina devastated Marsalis's hometown of New Orleans. He became very active in raising money to help the people of the city. He's performed benefit concerts and brought the attention of the nation to the problem.

CURRENT WORK: Marsalis is currently writing a piece for the "Gospel Jazz Festival" held at Lincoln Center. It is in honor of the 200th anniversary of the Abyssinian Baptist Church in Harlem, one of the first African-American churches in the country. It is a tribute to the church, and to his deep belief in the importance of African-American culture.

He's also continuing to produce shows for Jazz at Lincoln Center Radio. It is an award-winning series heard every week on public radio stations.

WYNTON MARSALIS'S HOME AND FAMILY: Marsalis lives in New York City. He has never been married. He has three sons, two with Candace Stanley, Wynton Jr. and Simeon, and one with Victoria Rowell, Jasper.

HIS LEGACY: Marsalis is devoted to bringing the importance and joy of jazz music to people all over the world. In his programs at Lincoln Center, his concerts, and workshops, he wants to instill in people an appreciation for the form of music he loves.

WORLD WIDE WEB SITES:

http://www.sonymusic.com
http://www.jazzatlincolncenter.org/
http://www.wyntonmarsalis.org/biography/
http://www.jazzworld.com/Artist_Info/wyntonmarsalis/

Toni Morrison

1931 -

African-American Writer

First Black Woman to Win the Nobel Prize in Literature

TONI MORRISON WAS BORN on February 18, 1931, in Lorain, Ohio. Her name when she was born was Chloe Anthony Wofford. (She changed her name from "Chloe" to "Toni" when she was older.) Her parents were Ramah and George Wofford. She was the second of four children.

TONI MORRISON GREW UP in a loving, hard-working family. She was born during the Great Depression. That was a time in the 1930s when up to 25% of Americans couldn't find work. Toni's father sometimes worked three jobs to keep his family fed and clothed.

Lorain was an integrated, working-class town. Morrison remembered that it was "an escape from stereotyped black settings. Neither plantation nor ghetto." Still, she faced racial discrimination as a child. She was raised among children of immigrants, and they always made her feel inferior.

A FAMILY OF STORYTELLERS: The Morrison family was close. They loved to entertain one another with stories. Many of them were based on African-American folk tales. Toni loved her father's stories, particularly his ghost stories. "We were always begging him to repeat the stories that terrified us the most," she remembered. These tales would influence her finest work.

TONI MORRISON WENT TO SCHOOL at the local public schools. She was always an outstanding student. She loved to read and explore the meaning of literature of all kinds. "Those books were not written for a little black girl in Lorain, Ohio," she recalled. "But they were so magnificently done that I got them anyway. They spoke to me directly."

Morrison graduated with honors and went on to college at Howard University. That is one of the finest traditional black colleges in the country. She majored in English. She enjoyed performing in the college theater group, the Howard University Players.

Morrison graduated from Howard in 1953. She went on to graduate school at Cornell University. She received her Master's degree in English in 1955.

TEACHING, WRITING, AND WORKING: Morrison's first teaching job was at Texas Southern University. She worked there for two years, then accepted a teaching position at Howard, her former college. In 1958, she married an architect named Harold Morrison. They soon had two sons.

In 1964, Morrison's marriage ended. With her young sons, she took a job in Syracuse, New York, as an editor for Random House. She worked as a book editor for the next 25 years, editing during the day, and writing at night. "I had two small children in a strange place and was very lonely," she recalled. "Writing was something for me to do in the evenings, after the children were asleep." After working in Syracuse for several years, she moved to New York City. Still working full time, she managed to finish, and publish, her first novel.

FIRST NOVELS: Morrison's first novel is called *The Bluest Eye*. It was published in 1969. Like all of her books, it deals with racism and its effect on African-Americans. And like most of her books, it is a very adult story, though its main character is a child. It is the story of a little girl who desperately wants what black children rarely have—blue eyes. The book explores the humiliations blacks suffer in white-dominated society.

Morrison kept up her busy schedule of editing books and writing book reviews, while writing more novels. Her novels from this time include *Sula* and *Song of Solomon*. In her editorial work, she edited the work of many African-American writers, including Muhammad Ali.

BELOVED: Morrison was working on an African-American history book when she came across a real-life story. It was about a

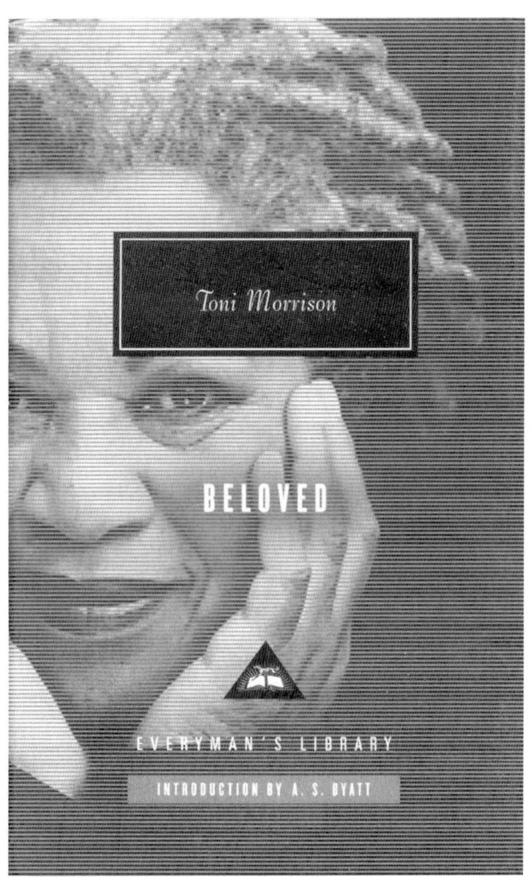

runaway female slave during the Civil War. The woman was caught, with her infant daughter, fleeing to freedom. The woman knew she and her baby would be forced to return to slavery. Rather than see her daughter raised a slave, the mother kills her baby.

That tragic, horrifying story became the basis for Morrison's best-known book, *Beloved.* In her novel, the mother, Sethe, is haunted by her murdered daughter, who returns as a ghost. Morrison says she wrote the book to remember the lives of the millions of slaves who died in this country. Slavery and its legacy is the curse that, like Beloved, haunts the novel, and American history.

In 1989, Morrison accepted a teaching position at Princeton University. From that point on, she has devoted her time to teaching and writing.

THE NOBEL PRIZE: In 1993, Morrison received the Nobel Prize in Literature. That is the greatest honor an author can receive. She was the first black woman to receive the award. The Nobel committee praised her "richly expressive depictions of Black America." Morrison was honored and overwhelmed by the prize. She gave a moving speech when she accepted the award. Soon, she was back at work, publishing more novels.

REMEMBER: In 2004, Morrison published another powerful book, this time for children. It's called *Remember: The Journey to School Integration*. It's the story of **BROWN V. THE BOARD OF EDUCATION** and the integration of the public schools.

That landmark case, argued by Thurgood Marshall before the U.S. Supreme Court, ended legalized segregation. (You can read about Marshall and the Brown case in *Biography for Beginners: African-American Leaders, Vol. 1.*) Morrison's book is a moving tribute to the courage of those who fought for the end of segregation. But it also shows the bravery of the children, many of them elementary age, who bravely confronted the racist people who didn't believe they were equal. It is a powerful and wonderful book.

Morrison continues to write and teach. She takes both very seriously. When she's writing, she likes to get up early "before there is light," she says. "I write with pencil, yellow pads, words, scratchings out."

She says that the planning process behind a book takes a long time. "I've spent a couple of years, just thinking about these people, the circumstances, the whole architecture of the book. I sort of feel so intimately connected with the place and the people and the events that when language does arrive, I'm pretty much ready."

TONI MORRISON'S HOME AND FAMILY: Toni Morrison married her husband, Harold Morrison, in 1958. They had two sons, Harold and Slade. They divorced in 1964. Harold and Slade are grown up now, and have children of their own.

HER LEGACY: Morrison is considered one of the finest writers of her generation, black or white, male or female. In 2006, *Beloved* was chosen as the best novel of the last 25 years. The power and beauty of her work isn't defined by race, although that is often her theme. Instead, she writes about the love, hope, and beauty of life, for all people.

WORLD WIDE WEB SITES:

http://nobelprize.org/
http://voices.cla.umn.edu/vg/Bios/entires/morrison_toni.html

Walter Dean Myers
1937 -
African-American Author of Books for Children and Young Adults

WALTER DEAN MYERS WAS BORN on August 12, 1937, in Martinsburg, West Virginia. His name when he was born was Walter Milton Myers. His parents were George and Mary Myers. Walter was one of seven kids.

Walter's mother died when he was two. His father was too poor to care for Walter and all his siblings. So when Walter was three, his dad turned to Florence and Herbert Dean for help. They became Walter's foster parents. They took him to New York City, where he grew up.

Myers loved his foster parents very much. The Deans gave him a warm, loving home. Later, when he became a famous writer, he changed his middle name to "Dean" to honor them.

WALTER DEAN MYERS GREW UP in Harlem, a mostly black area of New York City. He has many memories of growing up. He remembers playing stick ball and kick-the-can. He and his friends would play basketball all day and night.

Even though his family was poor, he felt loved and safe. He remembers a neighborhood where people watched out for one another. Sometimes, they just watched. The "Window Watchers" were ladies who spent their days at their windows to "watch what was happening on the block," he recalled. They'd report you to your mother right away if they saw you doing anything wrong.

Myers also remembers that the local church played a big part in his life. "I belonged to the Presbyterian church on the corner of my block," he recalls. "And the church and its teachings belonged to me as well. The church was just an extension of our homes. We drew our values, and our strengths, from that community and that church. It told us that life was good, and so were we."

LEARNING TO READ: Myers was taught to read by his foster mother when he was only four years old. Florence Dean could barely read herself, but she knew how important reading was.

She would read stories to him from *True Romance* magazine. It was filled romantic love stories. "I loved them," Myers recalls. "I didn't always understand them, but they were fun." They moved on to newspapers and even Classic Comic books. "Eventually, I was able to read to her," he recalls. "This was one of the greatest periods in my life with this woman."

WALTER DEAN MYERS WENT TO SCHOOL at the local public schools in Harlem. He was very bright, but he had a terrible speech problem. He could hardly be understood when he spoke. Other kids made fun of him. Myers fought back—with his fists. He became, he says, "a behavior problem."

But his teachers didn't give up on him. He remembers his fifth grade teacher, Mrs. Conway. "I had been suspended for fighting in class and had to sit in the back of the class while I waited for my mother to appear. The teacher, known for her meanness, caught me reading a comic under the desk."

She tore up the comic. "I was really upset, but then she brought in a pile of books from her own library," he recalled. "That was the best thing that ever happened to me."

"Books took me, not so much to foreign lands and fanciful adventures, but to a place within myself that I have been exploring ever since." Then he discovered the local library. "The public library was my most treasured place. I couldn't believe my luck in discovering that what I enjoyed most—reading—was free."

Myers continued to have problems speaking. One of his speech teachers suggested that he start writing, then try to read his work aloud. "I began writing little poems, and they helped me because of the rhythms. I began to write short stories, too."

Even though he won praise for his writing, he didn't think about becoming an author. "In fact," he says, "I didn't know there was such a job as an author."

He did know that school was not for him. He lost interest and dropped out at 15. He went back briefly, but became discouraged. Finally, at 17, he left high school for good and joined the Army.

FIRST JOBS: After several years in the Army, Myers returned to New York. He worked a lot of different jobs over the next few years. He worked for the post office, as a shipping clerk, and for the state of New York.

While he was working, Myers went back to school. He took college courses over the years and finally graduated in 1983.

He started to write again, too. Myers sent stories to magazines, and some of them got published. His big break came in 1968 when he entered a contest for black writers of children's books.

STARTING TO WRITE FOR KIDS: Myers sent in what became his first book, *Where Does the Day Go?* to the writing contest. To his surprise and delight, he won. The book was published and he was on his way.

Next, Myers sent a story about a group of teenagers to publishers. One editor thought it was a chapter from a book, and wanted him to write a whole novel. So, Myers recalls, "I made up the novel on the spot." That was his first book for teenagers, *Fast Sam, Cool Clyde, and Stuff.*

Since then, Myers has written more than 50 books for readers of all ages. Older kids love his novels that deal with the real issues teenagers face. One of his most popular recent young adult novels is *Monster.* It tells the story of a teenager in jail and on trail for

murder. Myers handles this painful story with realism and compassion.

Two of Myers's most popular books for younger readers are *Harlem* and *The Blues of Flats Brown.*

HARLEM: In 1997, Myers published one of his most popular books for young readers, *Harlem.* The book is actually a poem. It is about the sounds and sights of life in Harlem. It is filled with beautiful pictures painted by his son, Christopher. The poem and the pictures tell a tale of a city with a rich history of music and art. One line talks about "the artist looking into a mirror, painting a portrait of his own heart."

THE BLUES OF FLATS BROWN: Another favorite with early readers is *The Blues of Flats Brown.* It tells the story of two dogs, Flats and Caleb, who live with a mean junkyard owner. Flats can really play the blues guitar. But the junkyard owner has other plans. He wants to turn Flats and Caleb into fighting dogs. Flats and Caleb escape. But the owner catches up with them, first in Memphis, then in New York City. Through his music, Flats reaches the junkyard man. Finally, he leaves the dogs alone. In the last scene of the book, Flats and Caleb are playing music down near the waterfront in Savannah, Georgia.

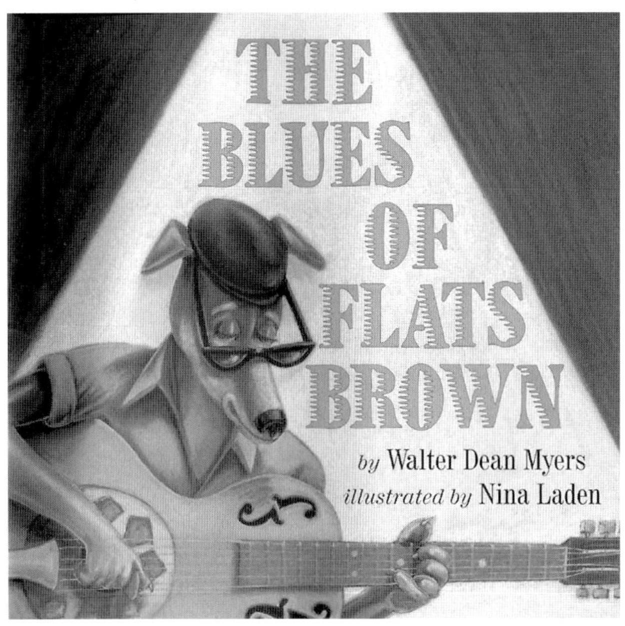

Myers has also written books on historical subjects for young readers. Some of these, like *Malcolm X: A Fire Burning Brightly* and *I've Seen the Promised Land: Martin Luther King*, are biographies of famous African-Americans. He's also published collections of photographs of children accompanied by poems.

ON WRITING: "I so love writing," says Myers. "It is not something that I am doing just for a living. It is something that I love to do." He starts his day with an early walk. Then he gets down to work.

He sets himself a goal of ten pages a day. He says that he "rushes through a first draft." Then, he goes back and rewrites. "Rewriting is more fun for me than writing," he claims.

WHERE DOES HE GET HIS IDEAS? Myers says most of his ideas come from his own life. "I write a lot about basketball, and I've played basketball for years and years. I lived in Harlem, and I write about Harlem. I'm interested in history, so I write about historical characters in nonfiction."

Recently, Myers returned to the subject of Harlem again. In *Here In Harlem: Poems in Many Voices* he celebrates the vital, colorful place that's meant so much to him.

WALTER DEAN MYERS'S HOME AND FAMILY: Myers has been married two times. His first wife was named Joyce. They married in 1960 and had two children, Karen and Michael. They divorced several years later.

Myers married again in 1973. His wife's name is Constance and they have one son, Christopher. He was the artist who did the beautiful pictures for *Harlem* and for *Jazz,* too. Myers and his wife live in New Jersey.

HIS LEGACY: Walter Dean Myers is one of the most popular and honored writers for young people in the U.S. His books have won many awards, including the Newbery Honor and the Coretta Scott King Award. He takes his job—and his readers—very seriously. "What I want to do with my writing is to make connections—to touch the lives of my characters and, through them, those of my readers."

WORLD WIDE WEB SITES:

http://www.scils.rutgers.edu/~kvander/myers.html
http://www.eduplace.com/kids/hmr/mtai/wdmyers.html
http://www.walterdeanmyers.net/

Gordon Parks

1912 - 2006

African-American Photographer, Author, Film Director, and Composer

GORDON PARKS WAS BORN on November 30, 1912, in Fort Scott, Kansas. He was the youngest of 15 children. His parents were Andrew and Sarah Parks. They were farmers. When Gordon was born, his heart wasn't beating. The doctor plunged him into cold water, and he survived. He was named after the man who saved his life, Dr. Gordon.

GORDON PARKS GREW UP in a poor but loving family. His parents taught him to value equality and the truth. However, the town he lived in was segregated. Gordon grew up at a time when black people did not have the same rights as white people. Blacks could not buy houses or find jobs where they wanted. In most places, they couldn't use the same buildings as white people. Blacks had to use different restaurants, movie theaters, even drinking fountains. They went to segregated schools.

GORDON PARKS WENT TO SCHOOL at the local public schools. His mother died when he was 15. It was a time of great sadness and change. He was sent to live with an older sister and her husband in St. Paul, Minnesota. However, he had a quarrel with his brother-in-law and had to leave the house. He never finished high school. Soon, he was homeless and in need of a job.

EARLY JOBS: Parks's mother had taught him to play piano. In St. Paul, he found work playing piano in a bar and singing in a band. He also worked as a waiter and mopped floors. When the band left for New York City, Parks followed them. He lived in the black neighborhood of Harlem and struggled to find work.

In 1933 Parks took a job with the Civilian Conservation Corps. That was a federal program that found work for people on public-service projects. This was during the Great Depression. It was a time when up to 25% of the population was out of work.

In 1933 Parks married Sally Alvis. He decided to return to St. Paul. In 1934 the couple had a son, Gordon Parks Jr. They would have two more children, a daughter, Toni, and a son, David.

Parks worked at various jobs to support his family. He was a busboy and a waiter, and briefly a semi-pro basketball player. In 1937 he took a job as a waiter on a train. That job would lead to a new career.

Parks at the office of the Farm Security Adminstration, 1943.

On a train bound for Seattle, Parks picked up a magazine left by a passenger. It included a photo essay of migrant workers. (Migrant workers are seasonal workers who move around the country doing farm work and other jobs.) The photographers who took the pictures worked for the Farm Security Administration (FSA). That was a Depression-era agency that hired photographers and writers to show how people were living around the country.

In Seattle, Parks bought his first camera. He took some pictures at the Seattle waterfront. Back home in Minnesota, he dropped the film off at a camera store to be developed. The manager was impressed with his work and displayed the photos.

A CAREER IN PHOTOGRAPHY: Parks began to find work in St. Paul as a fashion photographer. His photos were noticed by Marva

Louis. She was the wife of heavyweight boxing champion Joe Louis. Marva encouraged Parks to move to Chicago. He started to work in Chicago's South Side neighborhood. He did fashion photography, but also took photo's of life in the city's slums.

Parks's photos won him a Julius Rosenwald Fellowship. It paid him $200 per month. It also allowed him to choose a new career. Parks decided to move to Washington, D.C. He went to work in 1942 for the FSA's photography section. The staff included some the country's best photographers.

"AMERICAN GOTHIC": On his first day in Washington, Parks took one of his most famous photographs. He called it "American Gothic, Washington, D.C." It shows an African-American cleaning woman, Ella Watson, posed with her broom and mop in front of an American flag.

It seemed like a simple photo. But the story behind it wasn't simple at all. Watson's life was full of grief. Her mother had died and her father had been killed by a lynch mob. Her husband was accidentally shot to death two days before their first child was born.

Parks's choice of the name of his famous photo is important, too. It recalls a famous painting by Grant Wood, "American Gothic." That painting shows an old farm couple, with a pitchfork, in front of their barn. Park's photo shows, with compassion and concern, another American life, the life of an African-American.

After the FSA closed in 1943, Parks worked briefly for the Office of War Information. World War II had begun for the U.S. in 1941. One of his assignments was to cover the 332nd Fighter Group. That

Photograph of Ella Watson, with her daughter and three grandchildren, taken by Parks, 1942.

was the first unit of black fighter pilots in the U.S. Then, someone in the government decided he couldn't cover the story. Parks decided to quit his job and move back to Harlem.

COMMERCIAL SUCCESS: Parks again looked for work in the world of fashion photography. He faced prejudice again, when the magazine *Harper's Bazaar* wouldn't hire him because he was black. But the world-famous photographer Edward Steichen came to his aid. Steichen had seen Parks's work. He recommended him to the editors of *Vogue* and *Glamour* magazines. By the end of 1944, Park's photos had appeared in both publications.

***LIFE* MAGAZINE:** In 1948 Parks was hired to work for *Life* magazine. At that time, *Life* was one of the most popular magazines in the country. He was the magazine's first black staff photographer. He continued to work for them until 1972, logging more than 300 assignments.

During that time he covered everything: celebrities, urban crime, poverty, poetry, and the **CIVIL RIGHTS MOVEMENT.** Sometimes he wrote essays to go along with his photos. Over the years, his subjects included musicians **Louis Armstrong** and **Duke Ellington,** writer **Langston Hughes**, boxer Muhammad Ali, and Black Muslim leader Malcolm X. He also covered the high-fashion world, and was sent on assignments to Italy, Spain, Portugal, and Brazil.

THE LEARNING TREE: In 1963 Parks wrote an autobiographical novel, *The Learning Tree*. It was based on his early life. *The Learning Tree* was a great success, and was translated into several languages. In 1968, he began a movie career, producing and directing the movie version.

Parks was the first African-American to direct a movie for a major Hollywood studio. He followed *The Learning Tree* with another hit, *Shaft*. This 1971 movie was a huge commercial success.

Parks continued to produce movies and television documentaries. He also continued his writing and photography. He wrote two more autobiographical works and several volumes of poetry, accompanied by photographs. He was a cofounder of the magazine *Essence.* He also composed classical and the blues music. In 1989 he wrote the musical score and libretto for a ballet, *Martin.* It is a tribute to the life of Dr. Martin Luther King, Jr. Parks published several collections of his photographs. In 1998 he donated 227 pieces of his work to Washington's Corcoran Gallery of Art. In the 1990s he experimented with new methods in photography, including computerized techniques.

Gordon Parks died in his New York City home on March 7, 2006. He was 93 years old. His funeral was attended by hundreds of mourners. Many were photojournalists he had inspired.

GORDON PARK'S HOME AND FAMILY: Parks was married three times. He and his first wife, Sally, were married in 1933. They had three children, Gordon Jr., Toni, and David. They divorced in 1961. In 1962 Parks married Elizabeth Campbell. The couple had one daughter, Leslie, and were divorced in 1973. Parks married Genevieve Young in 1973. They divorced in 1979.

HIS LEGACY: From humble beginnings and with little education, Gordon Parks rose to become one of the most famous and productive artists of his time. He didn't let anything stand in his way. He found his vision and his voice, discovered untapped talents, and was unafraid to venture into new areas.

Parks was honored in his lifetime with 45 honorary degrees. In 2002 he was inducted into the International Photography Hall of Fame and Museum. That same year, he received the Jackie Robinson Foundation Lifetime Achievement Award. He is remembered as an artist who expressed his deeply-held beliefs in his photographs. "I chose my camera as a weapon against all the things I dislike about America—poverty, racism, discrimination. I could have just as easily picked up a knife or a gun. But I chose not to go that way. I felt that somehow I could subdue these evils by doing something beautiful that people recognize me by."

WORLD WIDE WEB SITES:

http://www.gordonparkscenter.org/
http://library.pittstate.edu/spcoll/ndxparks.html

Jerry Pinkney

1939 -

African-American Artist and
llustrator of Books for Children
Illustrator of *Mirandy and Brother Wind,*
The Talking Eggs,* and *Goin' Someplace Special

JERRY PINKNEY WAS BORN on December 22, 1939, in Philadelphia, Pennsylvania. His parents were James and Williemae Pinkney. James worked for a grocery store and did home repairs. Williemae was a homemaker. Jerry was the fourth of six kids. His brothers are named Eddie and Billy, and his sisters are Joan, Claudia, and Helen.

JERRY PINKNEY GREW UP in a loving, close family. His neighborhood was called Germantown. There were people from many backgrounds in his neighborhood: African-American, Italian, and Jewish.

Jerry was very close to his family, especially his cousins. When he was little, his aunt and uncle bought some property in the country. He and his cousins spent many days helping out building their house. They spent many nights sleeping out under the stars.

JERRY PINKNEY WENT TO SCHOOL at the local public schools. He loved drawing from the time he was little. He was good at it, too. At Hill Elementary School, he was considered the class artist. He says he wasn't very good at reading or spelling, but his art work won him praise.

By the time he was 11 or 12, Pinkney began to think about becoming an artist. He had a newspaper stand on a Philadelphia street corner. He'd take his sketch pad and draw while he waited for customers. A local artist named John Liney noticed his work. Liney was a successful cartoonist. He inspired Pinkney to become an artist.

"He took me to his studio," remembers Pinkney. Liney gave him art supplies and lots of encouragement. "At that early age I had a sense that it was possible to make a living doing art," Pinkney recalls. "Knowing him and seeing how he worked helped me understand the possibilities of using one's talents."

Pinkney went to Roosevelt Junior High, then to Dobbins Vocational High School. At Dobbins, he took courses in drawing and painting. He learned to use different techniques and materials. After high school, he went to college.

Pinkney won a scholarship to the Philadelphia Museum College of Art. He started college planning to use his art background to work in advertising. But he became more interested in painting. While he was in college, Pinkney got married and started a family. He left school after three years to earn money to support his family.

FIRST JOBS: Over the next few years, Pinkney worked as a delivery truck driver and flower arranger. Next, he got a job designing cards for a greeting card company.

After several years designing cards, Pinkney worked for a commercial art studio. While working for the studio, he received his first illustrating assignment.

BECOMING AN ILLUSTRATOR: Pinkney's first illustrated book was *The Adventures of a Spider.* It was written by Joyce Arkhurst and published in 1974. It's a collection of West African folk tales. Illustrating that book helped Pinkney decide on his career.

"My eyes were opened to the world of books," he recalls. "I can still remember, after months of work, waiting for the printed book to arrive. And when it did arrive, the touch, the scent, and the sound of opening a book for the first time. I knew at once that this is what I wanted to do."

In the next few years, Pinkney started his own business. He designed ads and illustrated books whenever he could. He became known as one of the finest illustrators of books for young readers.

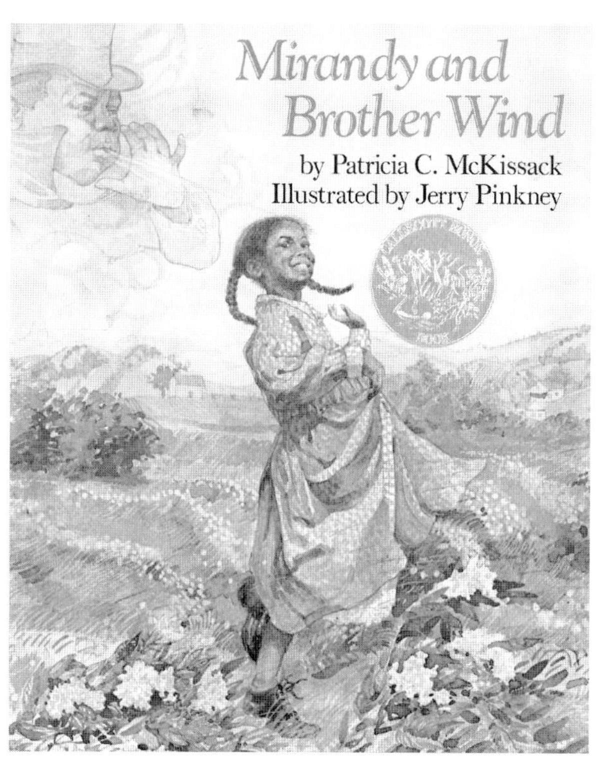

Over the years, Pinkney has illustrated many prizewinning books that are favorites with children. Among these are *The Patchwork Quilt, John Henry, The Talking Eggs, Mirandy and Brother Wind, Minty: A Story of Harriet Tubman*, and *Goin' Someplace Special.*

Pinkney is known for his vivid watercolor illustrations. He always does a lot of research for his illustrations. If he's doing a book set in another time, he'll study the way people looked and dressed. He uses live models. He has them dress in costumes, then photographs them. Using the photos, he begins his illustrations. First he makes pencil sketches, then adds the colors.

"I have to see the action in my head first," he says. "And then if I can see it in my head, it's very easy for me to find it in myself."

Pinkney has used his wife and children as models. Sometimes he's been a model, too. In books like *Further Tales of Uncle Remus*, you can recognize his face in the lion. "I actually become the people I'm drawing," he says. "And I do that with animals, too."

In addition to his book illustrations, Pinkney has done work for *National Geographic* magazine. He's also designed stamps used by the U.S. Post Office. And he's had collections of his art work shown in museums.

The theme of his illustrations is often African-American life. He remembers that when he was growing up, there were few black children in books. He wanted to change that for African-American children, including his own. "I wanted to show that an African-American artist could make it on a national level in the graphic arts. I want to be a strong role model for my family and for other African-Americans."

CELEBRATING AFRICAN-AMERICAN LIFE: Two of Pinkney's best known books, *Tales of Uncle Remus* and *John Henry*, show how he celebrates African-American life and culture. Here is how he describes it:

"Brer Rabbit, the sly trickster, originated during slavery and was the first African- American folk hero. Slaves who wanted to get the better of their masters needed to be cunning and sly—hence the trickster role. However, later comes John Henry, a free man, whose strength and valor bring him fame. He was a strong folk hero for African-Americans, a symbol of all the working men who made a major contribution to the building of the roads and railroads in the mountains of West Virginia—a dangerous job for which many paid with their lives."

JERRY PINKNEY'S HOME AND FAMILY: Pinkney met his wife, Gloria, when he was in high school. They married in 1959 and have four children, Troy Bernadette, Jerry Brian, Scott Cannon, and Myles Carter. They also have several grandchildren.

The Pinkneys are all very creative. Gloria writes books and also designs clothes and jewelry. All the kids were encouraged to express themselves in art. Jerry Brian, who is called Brian, is a children's book illustrator, too. He remembers that after the family went to a concert, "we always came home and made pictures. It was a family activity."

A COLLABORATION CELEBRATING AFRICAN-AMERICAN MUSIC: Recently, the Pinkneys published a book that was truly a family effort. *Music from Our Lord's Holy Heaven* is a collection of hymns, gathered by Gloria Pinkney. Jerry, Brian, and Myles Pinkney all illustrated the volume, and Troy wrote the introduction. It is a celebration of the hymns that have been sung by African-Americans for generations.

Jerry and Gloria Pinkney live in Croton-on-Hudson, New York. Jerry works out of a studio in his home. It's a screened-in porch overlooking the woods. Pinkney enjoys all kinds of music, from jazz to classical. He often listens to jazz while he draws.

HIS LEGACY: In more than 75 books, Jerry Pinkney has celebrated the lives and culture of African-Americans. His books are admired by readers of all ages. He has won many awards for his books, including five Caldecott Honors and five Coretta Scott King awards.

He has indeed accomplished his goal of creating books for, and about, African-American children. He was at a showing of his work a few years ago when a young African-American boy came up to him and pulled on his pant leg. Pointing to one of Pinkney's paintings, he said, "I see myself in your picture."

WORLD WIDE WEB SITES:

http://falcon.jmu.edu/~ramseyil/jpinkney.htm
http://www.eduplace.com/kids/hmr/mtai/jpinkney.html
http://www.penguinputnam.com
http://www.readingrockets.org/books/interviews/pinkneyj

Sidney Poitier

1927 -

African-American Actor and Director
First African-American to Win the Academy Award for Best Actor

SIDNEY POITIER WAS BORN on February 20, 1927, on a boat that was headed to Miami, Florida. His parents were Reginald and Evelyn Poitier. They grew tomatoes in the Bahamas, a chain of tropical islands near Florida. They were taking a crop of tomatoes to market in Miami when Sidney was born. He was the youngest of seven children in his family.

SIDNEY POITIER GREW UP in the village of Cat Island, Bahamas. His family's small farm had no electricity. He spent his early years swimming, fishing, and catching turtles. By the mid-1930s, foreign tomato growers were no longer allowed to sell their crops in the United States. Sidney's family lost the main market for their products. They were forced to sell their farm.

When Sidney was 11, his family moved to the large city of Nassau, Bahamas. They were very poor and struggled to make ends meet. His father got a job selling cigars. His mother worked for a company that crushed rocks into gravel. Sidney and his siblings did odd jobs to help support the family.

Reginald Poitier kept his pride and dignity during these hard times. He would not let his children feel sorry for themselves. Sidney remembered his father's example throughout his acting career. "Every time I took a part, from the first part, from the first day," he recalled, "I always said to myself, 'This must reflect well on his name.'"

Sidney saw his first movie during his years in Nassau. It was a magical experience for the teenager. He believed that all of the action on screen was real. After the Western ended, he waited to see the cowboys and horses ride out the door of the theater. "When I told my friends what had happened, they laughed and they laughed and they said to me, 'Everything you saw was on film,'" Sidney remembered. "And they explained to me what film was. And I said, 'Go on.'"

SIDNEY POITIER WENT TO SCHOOL in Cat Island for four years. His formal education ended when he moved to Nassau. Instead of going to school, he had to work to help support his family.

Poitier in Lilies of the Field.

DISCOVERS ACTING: At the age of 16, Poitier moved to the United States. He lived in Miami with an older brother for a while. He also served in the U.S. Army for a year. Poitier eventually moved to New York City. He arrived with three dollars in his pocket. He slept on a bench in the bus terminal. Then he got a job as a dishwasher in a restaurant.

One day, Poitier saw an ad in the newspaper for the American Negro Theater. The theater was looking for black actors to appear in plays. Poitier had never considered becoming an actor. But he thought performing on stage sounded like an easy way to earn money.

Poitier went to an audition. The owner of the theater asked him to read some lines from a script. Poitier could barely read, and he spoke with a strong Caribbean accent. The theater owner got angry. He felt that the young man had wasted his time. He grabbed Poitier by the collar and threw him out of the theater.

Poitier was upset about this experience. But it inspired him to make some important changes in his life. He was determined to prove that he could be an actor. Poitier worked with a tutor to improve his reading skills. He imitated radio broadcasters to get rid of his accent. He also worked as a janitor at the American Negro Theater in exchange for acting lessons.

LAUNCHING A SUCCESSFUL CAREER: Poitier's hard work soon paid off. He started getting small roles in plays at the American Negro Theater. For example, he appeared in *Days of Our Youth* with the well-known singer and actor **Harry Belafonte** (see "Brief Biopraphies"). In 1946 he made his first appearance on Broadway in the Greek comedy *Lysistrata.* Poitier was so nervous that he mixed up his lines. Even so, critics gave him good reviews.

Poitier's success in the theater encouraged him to audition for movie roles. He arrived in the film capital of Hollywood, California, at an ideal time. Some people in the film industry were determined to help African-Americans gain equal rights in society. They believed that they could change people's attitudes by creating positive images for black characters on screen. This situation opened up important new movie roles for talented black actors. Poitier became the top choice for many directors who were hoping to break down racial barriers and increase audiences' respect for African-Americans.

Poitier's first major role came in the 1950 film *No Way Out.* He played a black doctor who works in an otherwise all-white hospital. When one of his patients dies, the doctor is accused of murder by the man's racist brother. Also appearing in the film were **Ossie Davis** and **Ruby Dee.**

Poitier's big break to stardom came in the 1955 film *Blackboard Jungle*. He played a student at a dangerous inner-city high school. He is forced to choose a side during a tense standoff between a gang leader and a teacher.

Poitier was nominated for an Academy Award as best actor for his performance in the 1958 film *The Defiant Ones*. He played an inmate who escapes from prison while handcuffed to a white inmate. The two men hate each other at first. But as the movie continues, they overcome their differences and come to understand and depend on each other.

A RAISIN IN THE SUN: In 1959, Poitier was cast in one of the most important plays ever written by an African-American, *A Raisin in the Sun*. Written by **Lorraine Hansberry,** the play opened on March 1, 1959, on Broadway. It was a tremendous hit. It was the first play on Broadway with an all-black cast and director. It was also the first to portray African-American life. The play's original cast included both Poitier and **Ruby Dee.** They went on to star in the successful film version of the play.

AN ACADEMY AWARD: In 1963 Poitier won the prestigious Oscar as best actor for his performance in the uplifting film *Lilies of the Field*. He was the first black person to be honored with a best actor or actress award from the Academy of Motion Picture Arts and Sciences.

Poitier receiving the Academy Award for Best Actor.

In the film, Poitier played Homer Smith. He is an American soldier stationed in Europe during World War II. He meets a group of nuns who believe that he has been sent by God to help them build a chapel. As Smith constructs the church, he also builds bridges across their differences in race and nationality.

Winning an Oscar made Poitier one of the most famous actors in the United States. He used his fame to promote equality for

African-Americans. Poitier was an active participant in the **CIVIL RIGHTS MOVEMENT** of the 1960s. He took part in several protest marches led by the famous Civil Rights leader Dr. Martin Luther King, Jr.

In 1967 Poitier gave outstanding performances in three different films. In *To Sir, with Love,* he played a high-school teacher who inspires his students. In *Guess Who's Coming to Dinner,* he played a brilliant scientist who is engaged to marry a white woman. At the time the film opened, marriage between black and white people was still illegal in many states. It helped many people think about interracial relationships in a more positive way.

Poitier's third film of 1967 was *In the Heat of the Night.* He played Virgil Tibbs, a smart, experienced, big-city police detective. Tibbs is sent to solve a murder in a rural area. He eventually earns

Poitier, Katharine Houghton, Katharine Hepburn, and Spencer Tracy, in Guess Who's Coming to Dinner?

the respect of the local sheriff and many others. The three successful films helped make Poitier one of the highest-paid actors in the country.

MOVING BEHIND THE CAMERA: During the 1970s, Poitier turned away from acting. He moved behind the camera to direct films instead. He got his first chance to direct with the 1972 film *Buck and the Preacher.* It was an unusual sort of Western that featured black heroes and white villains. Poitier stepped in when the original director quit. He enjoyed it and did a good job.

Poitier went on to direct several more films during the 1970s. Most of these films were comedies that featured black actors. In 1974 he directed *Uptown Saturday Night.* It was a funny take on gangster films that starred **Bill Cosby,** Harry Belafonte, and Richard Pryor. Poitier also directed the 1980 comedy *Stir Crazy,* starring Richard Pryor and Gene Wilder. It became one of the biggest box-office hits of its time.

Poitier returned to acting in the 1990s. He starred in the 1991 TV miniseries *Separate but Equal.* He played Thurgood Marshall, who was the lead lawyer in **BROWN V. THE BOARD OF EDUCATION.** Marshall was also the first African-American to serve on the U.S. Supreme Court. (You can read a profile of Marshall in *Biography for Beginners: African-American Leaders, Vol. 1.*)

Poitier also appeared in the 1992 spy movie *Sneakers* with Robert Redford. In 1997 he starred with Bruce Willis in the hit action movie *The Jackal.* Later that year, Poitier served as an ambassador to Japan from his home country, the Bahamas.

WRITING ABOUT HIS LIFE: Poitier has written two books about his life and career. His first book, *This Life,* was published in 1980. It covers his childhood in the Bahamas and his struggles to build a successful acting career in the United States. Book critics called it well-written, honest, and charming.

In 2000 Poitier published a second memoir, *The Measure of a Man: A Spiritual Autobiography.* In it, he shares many lessons that he learned during his journey to stardom. In 2007 the influential talk show host **Oprah Winfrey** made it one of her book club selections.

INSPIRING BLACK ACTORS: Poitier holds a very important place in the history of film. He was one of the first black actors to appear in major dramatic roles in Hollywood movies. He was also one of the first black stars to connect with white audiences. In this way, Poitier helped break down racial barriers and change people's attitudes toward African-Americans. He also served as a role model and inspiration for future generations of black stars, such as **Denzel Washington**.

The film industry has recognized Poitier's influential role with a number of prestigious awards. He received a lifetime achievement award from the American Film Institute (AFI) in 1992. In 1999 the AFI ranked him as number 22 on its list of the top 50 film legends of the twentieth century. He was the only black actor included on the list. In 2001 Poitier was inducted into the **NATIONAL ASSOCIATION FOR THE ADVANCEMENT OF COLORED PEOPLE (NAACP)** Hall of Fame. The following year he received a special Academy Award for lifetime achievement.

Poitier remained modest about his groundbreaking role in film history. He claimed that many of his career accomplishments came because he was in the right place at the right time. "I didn't understand the elements swirling around," he stated. "I was a young actor with some talent, an enormous curiosity, a certain kind of appeal. You wrap that together and you have a potent mix."

SIDNEY POITIER'S HOME AND FAMILY: Poitier married dancer Juanita Hardy in 1950. They had four daughters together: Beverly, Pamela, Sherri, and Gina. His first marriage ended in divorce in 1965. Poitier married actress Joanna Shimkus in 1976. They had two daughters together: Anika and Sydney. He and his wife divide their time between homes in Los Angeles and New York.

HIS LEGACY: Poitier is one of the most celebrated actors of his generation. Yet he has always been modest about his accomplishments."I suited [the film industry's] need. I was clearly intelligent. I was a pretty good actor. I believed in brotherhood, in a free society. I hated racism, segregation. And I was a symbol against those things."

WORLD WIDE WEB SITES:

http://www.pbs.org/wnet/americanmasters/database/poitier_s.html
http://www.kennedy-center.org/calendar/index
http://www.harpercollins.com/authors/13974/Sidney_Poitier

Paul Robeson

1898 - 1976

African-American Singer, Actor, and Activist

PAUL ROBESON WAS BORN on April 9, 1898, in Princeton, New Jersey. His parents were William and Maria Robeson. William, a Presbyterian minister, had been a runaway slave. Maria was from a Quaker family who were committed to **ABOLITION.** Paul was the youngest of five children. His siblings were William, Reeve, Ben, and Marian.

PAUL ROBESON GREW UP in a family that faced painful losses. When he was just six years old, Paul's mother died in a house fire. A few years later, his father lost his job as a minister. The family moved to Somerville, New Jersey. There, his father became a minister of the St. Thomas AME Zion Church.

PAUL ROBESON WENT TO SCHOOL at the local public schools. He was always an outstanding student. At Somerville High School, he was one of only two black students. He was on the debate team, football team, and acted, too. He graduated with honors and won a scholarship to Rutgers University.

Rutgers was then an almost all-white school. Robeson faced racism, but refused to let it stop him. When he tried out for the football team, the white players beat him up. Undiscouraged, he tried out and won a spot on the team. He went on to become Rutgers's first All-American player. He won a total of 15 varsity sports letters while at Rutgers.

Robeson was also an outstanding student. He graduated from Rutgers as valedictorian, with the highest grade point in his class. He gave the graduation speech to the class of 1919.

LAW SCHOOL AND PERFORMING: Robeson went on to Columbia Law School. While in law school, he started his performing career. He sang in the chorus of musicals and acted in plays. His performance at the Harlem YMCA was praised by members of the Provincetown Players. That group was headed by famous playwrights like Eugene O'Neill. Robeson was getting noticed.

While he was in law school, Robeson also played pro football to earn money. He graduated from Columbia with a law degree in 1923.

BRIEF LAW CAREER: Robeson got a job as an attorney with a New York law firm. But his law career was very brief. One day, he asked one of the secretaries to prepare a letter for him. She refused, because he was black. Robeson quit his job in protest.

PERFORMING CAREER: Robeson decided to begin a career as an actor and singer. He had already sung at Harlem's famous Cotton Club. The same year he left the law firm, Eugene O'Neill cast him in one of his plays. As the star of *All God's Chillun Got Wings*, Robeson was a huge success.

He next appeared in *The Emperor Jones*, one of O'Neill's best plays. He also began giving concerts. Audiences loved his deep baritone voice. His programs usually included spirituals and folk songs.

In 1928, Robeson appeared in the London production of *Showboat*. It was a Broadway musical written by Jerome Kern and Oscar Hammerstein. Robeson's performance made him a star. His interpretation of the song "Ol' Man River," was a sensation. Over they years, it became his signature song.

In London, Robeson began to give recitals and concerts. Fans adored him. Returning to the U.S., Robeson gave a concert in New York's famous Carnegie Hall.

Robeson won praise for his acting, too. He was especially famous for his performance in *Othello*. That Shakespeare play portrays the tragic life of a black military leader, who murders his wife out of jealousy. Robeson was magnificent in the role. He portrayed Othello many times over the years, in England and America. In

Robeson with Jose Ferrer in the Theater Guild production of Othello, *1944.*

New York, his production of the tragedy had the longest run for a Shakespeare play in Broadway history, almost 300 performances.

Robeson appeared in several films, too. He was cast as the lead in the film version of *Emperor Jones*, and also appeared in the film version of *Showboat.* Robeson always chose roles that provided a positive view of African-Americans. He turned down parts he thought portrayed blacks in negative, or stereotypical ways.

A TRIP TO THE SOVIET UNION: In 1934, Robeson traveled to the Soviet Union. It was a trip that would change his view of the world. He was impressed with the Soviet political system, because it promoted racial equality. He met great artists, like filmmaker Sergei Eisenstein. He became a great supporter of the Communist system, and the Soviet leader, Josef Stalin.

Robeson pitching in a softball game with other cast members from Othello, *Central Park, New York, 1944.*

BECOMING AN ACTIVIST: Over the years, Robeson became more interested in speaking out against racism and oppression. He learned 15 languages and traveled the world. In Africa, he met political and social leaders. He raised money to fight diseases and famine.

Robeson believed he had a duty to speak out. "The artist must take sides. He must elect to fight for freedom or slavery. I have made my choice. There is no alternative." Already a popular artist, he became a symbol of the fight against oppression everywhere.

In the U.S., he condemned racism and prejudice against African-Americans. He met with President Harry Truman about the problem of lynching. (The term "lynching" means the murder of an individual, usually by a vigilante group. The term is usually used to describe the violent murder of blacks by whites.)

Robeson in Othello, *with Uta Hagen, 1944.*

CONTROVERSY OVER LOYALTY TO THE U.S.: In the late 1940s, public opinion turned against Robeson. This was the era of the Cold War. After World War II (1939-1945), the Soviet Union and the U.S. became the two strongest nations in the world. They represented two very different political systems. The U.S. was a democracy; the Soviet Union was a Communist state. The two "superpowers" also had powerful nuclear weapons. The relationship between the two nations was very important. For more than 40 years, the hostilities between these two nations affected world politics.

When Robeson first traveled to the Soviet Union in the 1930s, there were many who thought Communism offered hope to the world. But from the mid-1930s to the mid-1950s, Stalin proved to be a brutal dictator. He was responsible for the deaths of millions of his own people.

In the U.S., anti-Communist furor reached into all levels of life and work. Robeson, despite what was known about Stalin, refused to condemn him or Communism. Some began to question Robeson's loyalty to the United States. He was condemned as anti-American. His passport was taken away, and he wasn't allowed to travel outside the country.

Robeson faced condemnation from many different groups. In 1949, a crowd in Peekskill, New York, started a riot at one of his performances. He was even condemned by the **NAACP**. Concert promoters shunned him and he couldn't find work. A friend from that time spoke about the way he was treated. "Paul Robeson was the most persecuted, ostracized, condemned black man in American, then or ever." Still, he spoke out against repression and racism.

Finally, in 1958, Robeson got his passport back. He left the country and toured the world for five years. He was welcomed by crowds of admirers. But the years of controversy had taken their toll. He returned to the U.S. in poor health.

LATER YEARS: When Robeson returned to the U.S. in 1963, he was ill and frail. He retired from public life. He lived with his sister in Philadelphia until his death on January 23, 1976.

PAUL ROBESON'S HOME AND FAMILY: Robeson met Eslanda Goode when he was in law school. She was a chemist. They married in 1921 and had one son, Paul Jr.

HIS LEGACY: Robeson is remembered as an outstanding performer and activist, committed to speaking out against injustice everywhere. He was celebrated, then condemned in his own country. Today, people are still trying to take the measure of this enormously talented man, as well as the forces that condemned him.

WORLD WIDE WEB SITES:

http://africawithin.com/bios/paul_robeson
http://bayarearobeson.org/
http://www.pbs.org.wnet/americanmasters/database/robeson_p.html
http://www.princeton.lib.nj.us/robeson/bio.html

Bill "Bojangles" Robinson

1878 - 1949

African-American Dancer and Entertainer

BILL "BOJANGLES" ROBINSON WAS BORN on May 25, 1878, in Richmond, Virginia. His parents were Maxwell and Maria Robinson. They both died when he was a baby. Very little is known about his early life. He was raised by his grandmother, who was very strict.

Bill "Bojangles" Robinson's name has an interesting history. His name when he was born was Luther Robinson. His brother was named Bill, and when they were young Luther forced Bill to give him his name. The former Bill became "Percy." No one is sure how Robinson got the nickname "Bojangles."

BILL "BOJANGLES" ROBINSON WENT TO SCHOOL at the local public schools in Richmond. It isn't certain how long he went to school. He probably ran away from home when he was six or seven. He wound up in Washington, D.C.

A LIFE IN TAP: By the age of six, Bill and a friend were dancing in bars for money. They also shined shoes. Within a few years, he had a reputation as a "hoofer"—a song-and-dance man.

In 1892, Robinson appeared in a show called *The South Before the War.* It was a "minstrel" show. In minstrel shows, the performers, black and white, appeared in blackface. That means they painted their faces with black makeup. The characters in minstrel shows were often stereotypes. The black characters were slow-witted, cheerful, and happy with their "place." Many people today think the style is degrading and racist.

Around 1902, Robinson started performing with a partner, George Cooper. The two toured as a successful "Vaudeville" act for years. Vaudeville was a style of entertainment from the early 20th century that featured acting, singing, dancing, and other popular entertainment. In Robinson and Cooper's act, Cooper played the "straight man," and Robinson played the clown.

On the road, Robinson faced the racism of **JIM CROW**. Hotels, restaurants, even the concert halls they performed in were segregated. Robinson often couldn't find a place to eat or sleep. Around this time he started to develop a gambling habit. Sometimes he would gamble away all his earnings. He also had a quick temper and got into fights. Sometimes he was arrested and spent a night in jail.

In 1908, the duo broke up. Robinson got an agent, Marty Forkins. Forkins helped Robinson become a popular solo act. That was very unusual for the time, especially for a black performer. Through Forkins's efforts, Robinson became a highly paid and famous performer.

Robinson dancing in a photo from 1933.

HIS DANCE STYLE: Robinson is considered an important innovator in tap dancing. When he started dancing, the most popular tap style was "buck and wing." In that style, the dancer uses a flat-footed movement. Robinson was different. He danced high on his toes, and moved his upper body in an elegant fashion. He dressed in an elegant fashion, too, wearing well-made suits to complement his moves.

LIVING IN HARLEM: Robinson moved to Harlem in 1928. He appeared in a popular musical show, *Blackbirds of 1928.* It had an all-black cast and played for all-white audiences. Robinson appeared in other musicals, including *Brown Buddies* and *The Hot Mikado.*

Robinson danced at Harlem's famed Cotton Club. He was such a popular artist, he was named the honorary mayor of Harlem. He also became the mascot of the New York Giants baseball team.

Robinson performing, 1933.

FAMOUS MOVIES: In 1930, Robinson moved to California. There, he made 14 movies. He became a movie star.

Robinson's most popular co-star was child actress Shirley Temple. The dancer and the little girl appeared in such hits as *The Little Colonel* and *Rebecca of Sunnybrook Farm*. One routine they did was especially popular. They would dance up and down stairs, beating a catchy rhythm with their feet. Audiences loved it. But in later years, these movies, too, were criticized by some viewers. They thought that Robinson symbolized the submissive servant, too much like a slave.

One of Robinson's last films was *Stormy Weather*. Made in 1943, it featured an all-black cast. His co-star was an up-and-coming actress named Lena Horne. She would go on to become one of the finest actresses of the era. He also appeared on popular TV shows, like Ed Sullivan's variety program.

Legend has it that Robinson also came up with the term "copasetic," meaning "just fine." As a tribute to him, a group of tap dancers named themselves "The Copasetics."

LATER YEARS: Robinson danced well into his sixties, still drawing admiring audiences. On his 61st birthday, he danced all the way down Broadway, from Columbus Circle to 44th Street. The people of New York loved it.

Robinson dancing with Shirley Temple in the 1935 film, The Little Colonel.

Robinson was also generous to those in need. He held more than 3,000 benefit performances in his life, giving the money to charities. Yet this generous man also had a hard time holding on to money. By the time of his death, he had spent or gambled away most of his money. He died of heart disease on November 25, 1949.

New Yorkers turned out in the thousands for his funeral, lining the streets to view his funeral procession. The students of Harlem got a half-day off from school to attend.

BOJANGLES ROBINSON'S HOME AND FAMILY: Robinson was married three times. He married Lena Chase in 1907. The marriage lasted one year. Around 1920, he married Fannie Clay. They divorced in 1943. In 1944, Robinson married his third wife, Elaine Plaines. He never had children.

HIS LEGACY: Bill "Bojangles" Robinson was one of the most popular entertainers of the 20th century. Though his acting style may seem out-of-touch with the modern era, his dance innovations are still considered important.

WORLD WIDE WEB SITES:

http://americaslibrary.gov/cgi-bin/jb_date.cgi?day=25month=05
http://artsedge.keenedy-center.org/exploring/harlem/faces/robinson
http://www.tapdance.org/tap/people/bojangle.htm

Madam C. J. Walker

1867 - 1919

African-American Businesswoman

First Female Self-Made Millionaire in the United States

MADAM C. J. WALKER WAS BORN on December 23, 1867, in Delta, Louisiana, along the Mississippi River. Her name at birth was Sarah Breedlove. Her parents were Owen and Minerva Breedlove. She was the fifth of their six children. Sarah had one sister, Louvenia, and four brothers, Owen Jr., Alexander, James, and Solomon.

Before Sarah was born, her parents and older siblings were slaves. They picked cotton on a large plantation owned by a white master. The Civil War ended slavery in America in 1865. Sarah was the first member of her family to be born free.

MADAM C. J. WALKER GREW UP on the former slave plantation where she was born. Her family continued picking cotton for pay after slavery ended. They were very poor and lived in an old shack. Her parents died when she was seven years old. Sarah then went to live with her older sister and her husband in Vicksburg, Mississippi.

Sarah's brother-in-law abused her. She got married at age 14 in order to escape from him. In 1885 she gave birth to a daughter, Lelia. Her husband, Moses McWilliams, died two years later. Then Sarah moved to St. Louis, Missouri. Her four brothers worked in the city as barbers. She took jobs cooking, cleaning, and doing laundry. She also married her second husband, John Davis. They separated after a few years.

SCHOOL: Sarah did not go to school as a child. She learned to read and write as an adult with the help of tutors. She also attended night school classes in business management.

STARTING HER OWN BUSINESS: In the 1890s Sarah's hair started falling out. Like many African-American women of that time, she styled her hair in a way that was very hard on her scalp. She divided her hair into sections, twisted them tightly, and wrapped them with string. She eventually got a scalp disease that resulted in hair loss.

Sarah tried many home remedies and commercial products designed to re-grow hair. None of them worked very well. She finally asked God to help save her hair. She claimed that God answered her prayer in a dream. "In that dream a big black man appeared to me and told me what to mix up for my hair," she said. "Some of the remedy was grown in Africa, but I sent for it, mixed it, put it on my

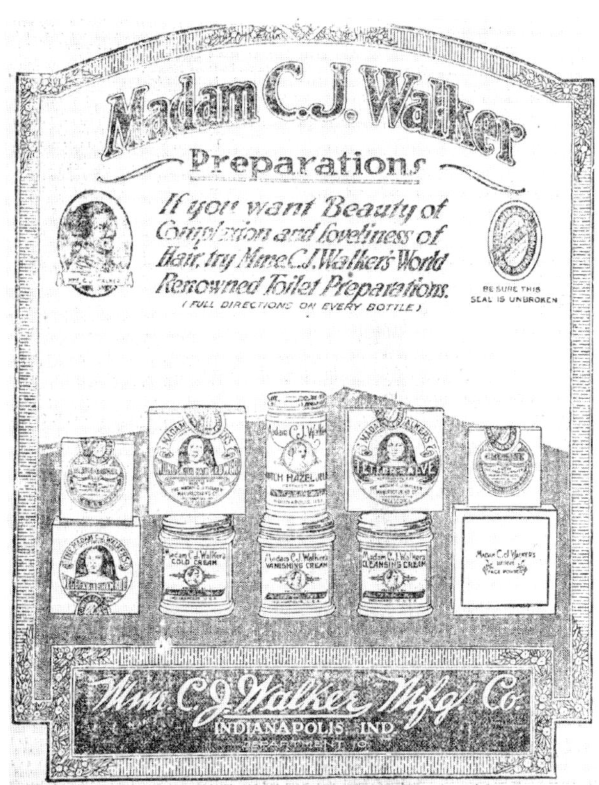

Advertisement for Walker's products, Jan. 17, 1920.

scalp, and in a few weeks my hair was coming in faster than it had ever fallen out."

Sarah decided to start a business selling hair products to black women. In 1905 she moved to Denver, Colorado. She married her third husband, a newspaper writer named Charles Joseph Walker. At this point Sarah changed her name to Madam C. J. Walker. She filled jars with a mixture she called Madam Walker's Wonderful Hair Grower. She demonstrated the product in churches and meeting halls and sold it door-to-door. Her husband helped her place newspaper advertisements and come up with marketing ideas.

BECOMING A MILLIONAIRE: Madam Walker worked hard to grow her business. She developed many new products and attracted many new customers. In 1908 she opened the Lelia College of Beauty Culture in Pittsburgh, Pennsylvania. She used this school to train African-American women to use and sell her products. Members of her company's sales force were known as "hair culturists."

In 1910 Walker built a factory in Indianapolis, Indiana, to manufacture her hair products. The success of the Madam C. J. Walker Manufacturing Company eventually made its founder very rich. In fact, Walker is listed in the *Guinness Book of World Records* as the first self-made American woman millionaire. This means that she earned a million dollars on her own, rather than inheriting a family fortune or marrying a wealthy man.

SUPPORTING CHARITY AND THE ARTS: In 1916 Walker moved to New York City. She continued to oversee her business operations from there. She and her daughter also became active supporters of the **HARLEM RENAISSANCE,** an African-American artistic and cultural movement that was happening at that time. They often hosted gatherings of some of the nation's best-known black writers, musicians, and entertainers.

In 1917 racial violence broke out in East St. Louis, Illinois. A white mob killed more than 30 African-Americans. Walker was very concerned about these events. She believed that the country needed strict new laws to prevent the murder of minorities. Walker joined a group of black leaders on a trip to Washington, D.C., that year. They visited the White House to ask the president to support such laws.

Stamp commemorating Walker's achievements, 1998.

Later that year, Walker held a meeting of all her saleswomen in Philadelphia, Pennsylvania. It was one of the first national conventions of businesswomen in the United States. Walker encouraged her sales force to be politically active and fight racial injustice. She set a good example by donating money to build recreation facilities, museums, and libraries for African-Americans.

SETTING NEW STANDARDS OF BEAUTY: Some people criticized Walker's beauty products. They claimed that some of the things she sold, like hair straighteners, made black people look more like white people. They felt that African-Americans should be proud of their natural appearance.

Walker defended her company's purpose. She said that she only wanted to help African-American women be healthy, well-groomed, and confident. "I have always held myself out as a hair culturist," she stated. "I want the great masses of my people to take a greater pride in their appearance and to give their hair proper attention."

LATER YEARS: Walker died of kidney failure on May 25, 1919, at the age of 51. She was buried at Woodlawn Cemetery in the Bronx section of New York City. The Madam C.J. Walker Manufacturing Company remained in business for another 75 years. Its product line was finally sold to another company in 1985.

MADAM C. J. WALKER'S HOME AND FAMILY: Walker was married three times. Her husbands were Moses McWilliams, John Davis, and Charles Joseph Walker. Her first husband died, and her other marriages ended in divorce. She had one daughter, Lelia (who later changed her name to A'Lelia), with her first husband. Walker lived at Villa Lewaro, an estate that she built in Irvington-on-Hudson, New York.

HER LEGACY: The story of Walker's life has inspired many people. She started a successful business at a time when business careers were not yet open to African-Americans or women. She also helped launch the entire industry of black hair-care and cosmetic products. In honor of her business success, Walker was inducted into the National Business Hall of Fame and the National Women's Hall of Fame.

Walker is also remembered for hiring and training thousands of black women to sell her products. These jobs gave the women a way to challenge themselves, become independent, and improve their place in society. "The girls and women of our race must not be afraid to take hold of business endeavors," Walker once said. "I have made it possible for many colored women to abandon the washtub for a more pleasant and profitable occupation."

WORLD WIDE WEB SITES:

http://www.madamecjwalker.com
http://www.greatwomen.org
http://www.ja.org/hof/past_laureates.shtml

Denzel Washington
1954 -
African-American Actor
Winner of Two Academy Awards

DENZEL WASHINGTON WAS BORN on December 28, 1954, in Mount Vernon, New York. His parents were Denzel Sr. and Lennis Washington. Denzel Sr. was a minister and Lennis was a gospel singer who ran several beauty shops. Denzel has a sister, Lorice, and a brother, David.

DENZEL WASHINGTON GREW UP in Mount Vernon, which is near New York City. His neighborhood was full of people from many different races and backgrounds. His parents were very strict. They insisted that Denzel and his sibling do well in school, and behave themselves, too.

He recalls that his Mom kept him from "becoming a sure-nuf gangster." "My mother's love for me and her desire for me to do well kept me out of trouble," he recalls.

DENZEL WASHINGTON WENT TO SCHOOL at the local public schools. When he was 14, his parents got a divorce. It affected him deeply. "I rebelled and got angry and started beating people up at school," he remembers. His Mom took action. She sent Denzel to the Oakland Academy. That's a small, private school in upstate New York.

Life was very different at Oakland. Washington says it was "very rich and very white." He didn't do particularly well in school, but he was a standout in sports. He played baseball, basketball, football, and ran track. He also played in the band.

After Washington graduated from Oakland in 1972, he went to college at Fordham University. He started out thinking he'd be a doctor, but changed his plans. One summer during college, he worked at a YMCA camp. He took part in a skit, and he loved it.

When he returned to college, Washington changed his major. He spent his final years studying theater and journalism. He started to appear in many different plays, from Shakespeare to modern works. As a senior, he got a great break. He landed a role in a TV movie based on the life of Wilma Rudolph. (Rudolph was an Olympic track star. You can read a profile of her in *Biography for Beginners: African-American Leaders, Volume 1.*)

After graduating from Fordham, Washington headed to California. He'd been accepted into an acting program in San Francisco. But after a year, he decided to move to Los Angeles to find acting work. Soon, he was back in New York, trying to find work in the theater.

EARLY CAREER AS AN ACTOR: Making a living as an actor was tough work, but Washington began to get parts. He worked for several years with small acting companies, performing a wide range of roles. When the work wasn't steady, he'd get discouraged, but he didn't give up. His wife, Pauletta Pearson, is also an actress. She encouraged him, and he stuck with it.

In 1981, Washington landed a key role. He played Pvt. Melvin Peterson in Charles Fuller's *A Soldier's Play*. The play was about a group of African-American soldiers in World War II, when the Army was segregated. Critics and audiences praised Washington's acting in the play. In 1984, it was made into a movie, *A Soldier's Story*. Washington appeared in the movie version, too, to great reviews. He was really beginning to get noticed.

In 1982, Washington won the role of Dr. Philip Chandler on the TV show *St. Elsewhere*. He was watched by millions of viewers every week, and his fame began to grow.

Washington in Spike Lee's Malcolm X.

Washington took on another important role in 1987, when he played South African activist Stephen Biko in *Cry Freedom.* He won his first Academy Award nomination for the role. And his success led to the most important part of his early career, in *Glory.*

GLORY: *Glory* is a Civil War film about the famous 54th Regiment. It was the first all African-American unit to fight for the Union. Its valor and bravery are legendary. Washington played a character named Trip, a fugitive slave. He worked hard researching the role, and his performance showed it. Washington won the Academy Award for Best Supporting Actor for his performance in *Glory.*

Washington next began to work with director **Spike Lee** on the film *Mo' Better Blues.* Lee wrote the part of Bleek Gilliam especially for Washington. The actor and director worked together again a few years later, on another important role for Washington.

MALCOLM X: In 1992, Washington played the fiery **Civil Rights** leader Malcolm X, in a film directed by Lee. Washington was brilliant in the role. He brought the passionate, controversial leader to life, and to the attention of a new generation. Washington received another Academy Award nomination for his performance.(You can read a profile of Malcolm X in *Biography for Beginners: African-American Leaders, Vol. 1.*)

Washington is an actor capable of a wide range of roles. In 1993 he showed that range. He appeared in a movie version of Shakespeare's *Much Ado about Nothing*. He co-starred with Julia Roberts in the crime thriller *The Pelican Brief*. And he co-starred with Tom Hanks in the award-winning film *Philadelphia*.

In the next few years, Washington continued to show his range and depth. He appeared as a Navy officer in *Crimson Tide*. He played a military role again as the army investigator in *Courage Under Fire*.

Washington showed he could do romantic comedy, too, starring with Whitney Houston in *The Preacher's Wife* in 1996. In 1999, with dramatic and athletic power, he portrayed boxer Hurricane Carter in *Hurricane*. Washington received his fourth Academy Award nomination for that performance.

Another favorite role from recent years is his portrayal of a high school football coach in *Remember the Titans* (2000). The film was based on the experiences of Herman Boone, who coached the first integrated football team in Virginia in 1971.

Washington as Don Pedro in Much Ado About Nothing, *with Kenneth Branaugh and Emma Thompson.*

A SECOND ACADEMY AWARD: In 2001, Washington played a corrupt cop in *Training Day*. His performance won him the Academy Award for Best Actor. He became only the second African-American, after **Sidney Poitier**, to be so honored.

STARTING TO DIRECT: Washington has moved behind the camera in the past few years. In 2002, he directed *The Antwone Fisher Story*. It's a true story of a Navy sailor who becomes a writer. Washington also starred in the film, as a compassionate therapist who reaches out to the troubled young Antwone Fisher.

RECENT FILMS: Washington has appeared in several recent films, including *The Manchurian Candidate* in 2004 and *American Gangster* in 2007.

Washington as coach Herman Boone in Remember the Titans.

In 2007, Washington directed and starred in *The Great Debaters*. The film is based on the story of an award-winning debate team from Wiley College, a small traditional black college in Texas. In the 1930s, Wiley's debate team won top honors against prestigious, white colleges from all over the country.

In the film, Washington plays the debate coach, Melvin Tolson, who leads his young students to the highest level, fighting racial prejudice with dignity and honor. The film is a moving tribute to their intelligence and courage. It was produced by **Oprah Winfrey**.

DENZEL WASHINGTON'S HOME AND FAMILY: Washington met his wife, Pauletta, when they were both cast in the TV movie *Wilma*. They married in 1983 and have four children. Their son John David, born in 1984, is a pro football player. Daughter Katia, born in 1987, is in college. Twins Olivia and Malcolm (named for Malcolm X) were born in 1991 and are in high school.

Washington as debate coach Melvin Tolson in The Great Debaters.

Washington is a devoted family man. He loves being a father and has always been very involved in his kids' lives. He also has great respect and admiration for his wife. "Pauletta's sacrificed a lot of opportunities. She was doing Broadway shows. She was a child prodigy, a concert pianist. She's competed in Van Cliburn competitions, and been all over the world. I told her I want her to do whatever she wants to do for her career. But she's really committed to family and to helping and supporting me. I don't know what I'd do without her. She's my foundation and my stability."

HIS LEGACY: Denzel Washington's legacy is still in the making. After almost 30 years in films, he still wants to grow in his art. He plans to continue to act, direct, and produce for many years to come.

Washington is committed to helping out those in need, too. He's a big supporter of Boys' Clubs, having benefitted from them himself. Recently, he was visiting a hospital for Americans wounded in the Iraqi war. He made a generous donation to the hospital, as a way of paying tribute to the soldiers and their sacrifice.

WORLD WIDE WEB SITES:

http://www.imbd.com
http://biography.com/kids

Phillis Wheatley

1753? - 1784

African-American Poet

First African-American to Publish a Book

PHILLIS WHEATLEY WAS BORN around 1753 in Gambia, Africa. No one is sure of her exact birth date or her original name. When she was around seven years old, she was captured from her African home and sold into **SLAVERY.** She was brought by a slave ship called *Phillis* to Boston. There, she was bought by John and Susannah Wheatley on July 11, 1761. They named her Phillis Wheatley.

PHILLIS WHEATLEY GREW UP in the Wheatley home. She was supposed to be a servant, but she was often in poor health. She was very intelligent, and learned English very quickly.

LEARNING TO READ AND WRITE: The Wheatleys discovered Phillis writing on a wall with chalk.They encouraged her to devote herself to learning. They taught her to read and write, and she thrived. She learned several languages, including Latin and Greek. She studied theology—the study of religion—and literature. She especially loved poetry.

STARTING TO WRITE POETRY: Soon Phillis began to write poetry of her own. One of her poems was published in 1767, in a Rhode Island newspaper. It was called "On Messrs. Hussey and Coffin."

Wheatley liked to write a form of poetry called an "elegy." An elegy is a poem celebrating the life and works of an individual, usually written at the individual's death. Wheatley showed her deep Christian faith and her admiration for Colonial leaders in these poems. They made her a very popular poet. Some of her work appeared as broadsides and were widely read.

Wheatley attended services at the Old South Church in Boston. When her minister, Joseph Sewall, died in 1769, she wrote an elegy commemorating his life. It was admired by many Bostonians.

In 1770, she published her most famous elegy, "On the Death of Mr. George Whitefield." Whitefield was an English minister who was well known in Colonial America. Wheatley's poem was read and celebrated in Boston and London. It caught the attention of a wealthy English admirer, the Countess of Huntingdon.

A TRIP TO LONDON: Wheatley sailed to England in 1773, hoping to meet the Countess. Although they were unable to meet, the Countess provided the money to publish Wheatley's first book of poetry.

PUBLISHING HER BOOK: Wheatley's first book, *Poems on Various Subjects, Religious and Moral,* was published in 1773. It was the first book ever published by an African-American. And it was only the second book of poetry ever published by an American woman. (The first was by Anne Bradstreet, an earlier Colonial American.)

BECOMING A FREE WOMAN: When Phillis returned from England, the Wheatleys freed her. She was a free woman at last.

Wheatley continued to write poems. In 1776, the colonies had declared war against England. Wheatley wrote a poem dedicated to General George Washington. He praised her verse and her support of the Revolutionary War. He also invited her to meet him. They did meet in 1776. Wheatley's poem on Washington was printed and distributed during the war, rallying Americans to the cause.

Wheatley was a strong supporter of the cause of independence, and liberty for all people. She also believed that slavery was a curse that Colonial Americans must confront. In one poem, she states that white people cannot "hope to find/Divine acceptance with th'Almighty mind" when "they disgrace/And hold in bondage Afric's blameless race."

Wheatley's letters also reveal her hatred of slavery. In a letter to a friend, she wrote: "In every human Breast, God has implanted a Principle, which we call Love of Freedom. It is impatient of Oppression, and pants for Deliverance."

Wheatley's last known poem was published in 1784, the year of her death. It was called "Liberty and Peace." In it, she celebrates the victory of the Revolution. She tried to find subscribers to pay for the publication of another collection of her poems, but died before she could find enough supporters. Tragically, her final manuscripts were never found.

PHILLIS WHEATLEY'S HOME AND FAMILY: Wheatley married John Peters in 1778. He was a free black man. He had a business, but it failed. The family struggled in poverty for several years. Phillis had to find work as a servant. She had three children, but, tragically, all died. Phillis Wheatley died on December 5, 1784, around the age of 30.

HER LEGACY: Wheatley is honored as the first African-American to publish a book in the U.S. Her poetry was admired for its religious and patriotic themes. She was a woman of great intelligence and poetic gifts. She used those gifts to praise God, and also to promote freedom for all.

WORLD WIDE WEB SITES:

http://americanslibrary.gov/cgi-bin/page.cgi/jb/revolut/poetslave_
http://www.pbs.org/wgbh/aia/part2/2p12/html

Oprah Winfrey

1954 -

African-American Television Talk Show Host, Producer, Publisher, Actress, and Entrepreneur

OPRAH WINFREY WAS BORN on January 29, 1954, in Kosciusko, Mississippi. Her parents are Vernon Winfrey and Vernita Lee. They were not married when Oprah was born, and she was raised by her grandmother. Her full name is Oprah Gail Winfrey.

Oprah's unusual first name is based on the name "Orpah," who is a woman in the Bible. No one is sure how the letters got mixed up, but she's been known as Oprah all her life.

OPRAH WINFREY GREW UP on a farm with her grandmother. She used to perform "plays" for the pigs and chickens. She was very bright and learned to read when she was three. She and her grandmother were regular church-goers. Oprah liked to recite Bible passages to the congregation.

When she was six, Oprah went to live with her mother in Milwaukee, Wisconsin. The next years were terrible for her. A male cousin and several other relatives sexually abused her. She was frightened and ashamed. She didn't know what to do. She didn't tell anybody, but she started to act out.

Oprah became rebellious and wouldn't listen to her mother. She stole money from her mom and ran away from home. Her mom didn't know what had happened to her. And she didn't know how to handle her daughter. So when Oprah was 14, her mom sent her to live with her dad and stepmother, Vernon and Velma Winfrey, in Nashville, Tennessee.

Her dad and stepmom were very strict. Oprah had to follow all their rules. In their home and under their guidance, she blossomed.

OPRAH WINFREY WENT TO SCHOOL first in Milwaukee then in Nashville. In Nashville, she attended East High School. Her dad expected her to do well in school, and she did. She joined the drama club and was president of the student council. She got a job at a local radio station. During her senior year, she won a speech contest. She used the cash prize to pay for college.

Oprah attended Tennessee State University in Nashville. There, she studied speech and drama. While still a student, Oprah started working at a local TV station. She became the first African-American woman to anchor the news in Nashville. She was only 19. And she also found the time to enter beauty contests. She won the Miss Black Tennessee title. Oprah graduated from Tennessee State in 1976.

STARTING A CAREER IN BROADCASTING: Oprah's first full-time job was with WJZ-TV in Baltimore. She co-hosted a talk show, "People Are Talking." She was a hit.

In 1984 Oprah moved to Chicago, where she hosted a morning show called "A.M. Chicago" on WLS-TV. In just one month her show jumped to Number One in the ratings. One year later, the show was renamed "The Oprah Winfrey Show."

"THE OPRAH WINFREY SHOW": Oprah's famous TV show has been a huge success since it first began. It has been the top-rated talk show for years. Every day, she talks to guests about many different topics. An important part of the show is the audience, who question the guests and comment on the topic. The show is watched by 26 million people each week. It appears in 106 countries around the world.

Oprah's show covers a wide range of things. Sometimes she'll have people on who talk about bullying and its effect on kids. Sometimes they'll cover stories in the news. Sometimes the show is about health and fitness.

In all her shows, Oprah encourages people to develop and achieve personal goals. Many of her shows focus on women, children, and education. She wants people to feel that they have what it takes to learn, to strive, and to achieve.

Winfrey's school for girls in South Africa.

One topic that is very important to her is child abuse. Since she was a victim herself, she wants to help protect children any way she can. Several years ago, she helped create federal laws to protect children against abuse.

In 1996, Oprah started the "Oprah Book Club." She encouraged people all over the country to read books, then she'd have the author on the show to discuss them. The program has been a great success. She's gotten millions of people to read and think about good books.

Oprah and her show have won many awards, too. To date, she's won 16 Emmy Awards. *Newsweek* magazine named her the "Woman of the Century." And she has been named to many lists of the most important people in the world of television.

Winfrey and David Zaslav announce the launch of "OWN: The Oprah Winfrey Network," Jan. 2008.

HARPO: Oprah produces her TV show through a production company called "Harpo." (That's "Oprah" spelled backwards.) In addition to her TV show, she has produced TV movies. These include *Their Eyes Were Watching God,"* written by **Zora Neale Hurston** and starring **Halle Berry**. Recently, she produced *The Great Debaters*, directed by and starring **Denzel Washington.**

ACTING: Oprah has also acted in several movies. In 1985, she played the character Sofia in *The Color Purple*. That performance won her an Academy Award nomination. In 1998, she appeared in the movie *Beloved*.

Winfrey and Bono shop to raise money for AIDS research, 2007.

She's also appeared in several TV movies. These include *The Women of Brewster Place*, *There Are No Children Here*, and *Before Women Had Wings.*

***O, THE OPRAH MAGAZINE*:** In 2000, Oprah started a new magazine. It's called *O, The Oprah Magazine*. Even though she's busy with her TV show, she reads and edits every page of the magazine. Like her other projects, it has been a great success.

ENTREPRENEUR: All of these business projects have helped make Oprah a successful "entrepreneur." An entrepreneur is a person who starts and develops a business. It is a person who is willing to take great risks to start something new. And that's Oprah. She doesn't seem daunted by any challenge. And the businesses she creates thrive.

GIVING BACK: Oprah thinks it's important to give back to the community. "You get from the world what you give to the world," she says. Her foundation has given away millions of dollars to programs to help others. Several are scholarship programs for needy kids.

In 1997, she created Oprah's Angel Network. She wanted to encourage people to help improve the lives of others. So far the Network has raised millions for people in need. The money has been used for many causes. It's helped to build Habitat for Humanity houses and fund college scholarships.

In 2007, Oprah opened The Oprah Winfrey Leadership Academy for Girls in Johannesburg, South Africa. The school educates 7th and 8th grade girls.

Oprah's TV show is still going strong. In January 2008, she announced that she would begin her own TV network, the OWN (Oprah Winfrey Network). She continues to be busy with television, movies, and her magazine. And she continues to give back to the world in which she's been such a success, to help people achieve their goals.

OPRAH WINFREY'S HOME AND FAMILY: Oprah lives in a large condominium in Chicago. She also has a farm in Indiana. She loves to spend time at her place in the country. She also loves to exercise, and she has a gym in her offices in Chicago. She also enjoys spending time with her boyfriend, Stedman Graham.

WORLD WIDE WEB SITE:

http://www.oprah.com

Richard Wright

1908 - 1960

African-American Novelist and Short Story Writer

RICHARD WRIGHT WAS BORN on September 4, 1908, near Natchez, Mississippi. His parents were Nathan and Ella Wright. Nathan was a farmer and Ella was a teacher. Richard had one brother, Leon.

RICHARD WRIGHT GREW UP in several places. He spent his first years in rural Mississippi. He loved to roam the woods. When he was six, the family moved from Mississippi to Memphis, Tennessee. His family was poor, and his parents hoped to find better-paying jobs.

In Memphis, Nathan Wright got a job as a night porter. Richard and his brother grew to hate Memphis, though. They missed playing outdoors in the countryside. Also, Richard grew to hate his father. He was a stern man. Richard couldn't even talk to him. "I never laughed in his presence," he recalled.

Despite their hard work, Richard's parents couldn't make enough money to put food on the table. He remembered being hungry all the time. "Hunger had always been more or less at my elbow," he recalled. "Now I began to wake up at night to find hunger standing at my bedside."

Richard's father left the family, and their poverty grew worse. His mother became ill, and Richard and his brother were sent to live in an orphanage. He remembered that each day he felt "hunger and fear." His mother got a little better, then had several strokes that left her permanently disabled. She and her sons moved in with relatives, first in Arkansas, then in Mississippi.

In Mississippi, they lived with Richard's grandparents. They were very religious, and their faith didn't allow children's games or sports. It was very hard for Richard. He began to rebel, and refused to follow his grandparent's rules.

By this time, Richard had begun to understand and feel the racism that was part of the daily lives of black people. It was the time of **JIM CROW**. Throughout the country, particularly in the South, blacks had few if any rights. The states passed laws that made segregation legal. It offered "separate but equal" facilities. But the facilities were anything but equal. Facilities—schools, restaurants, theaters—were segregated by race. Decent jobs, and good schools, were denied to African-Americans.

RICHARD WRIGHT WENT TO SCHOOL only occasionally, because he moved around so often. Still, he was a bright child. When he did get to school, he was promoted several grades. He loved learning, and he asked questions constantly. "I told the family I was going to study medicine, engage in research, make discoveries," he wrote later.

"I now saw a world leap to life before my eyes," he recalled. But his family didn't support his plans. When he told them he wanted to write, they said he was wasting his time. They thought he should accept his "place" as a black in white society. He refused.

MOVING ON: After finishing ninth grade, at age 17, Wright left Mississippi and moved back to Memphis. But once again, racism defined his life. He couldn't even get a library card to use the public library. He had to ask a white friend to let him use his name to get a library card.

FIRST JOBS: Wright decided to move to Chicago. He thought the north might provide more opportunity to him. He worked jobs during the day—as a busboy, a dishwasher, a street sweeper—and wrote at night. His mother and brother moved to Chicago to live with him.

Wright got a job at the Post Office to support his family. But he lost that job in the 1930s, during the Great Depression. That was a time of world-wide economic hardship. In the U.S., up to 25% of the population couldn't find work.

Wright was able to get a job with the Federal Writer's Project. That was a relief program started during the Depression to provide aid to unemployed writers. While working for the government, he continued to write his own work, too.

UNCLE TOM'S CHILDREN: In 1938, Wright published his first work of fiction. Called *Uncle Tom's Children*, it was a collection of stories about racism and African-American life. Wright took his title from a famous 19th-century novel, *Uncle Tom's Cabin*. That work, by **ABOLITIONIST** Harriet Beecher Stowe, portrayed the life of blacks under slavery. Wright's book showed how the horrible legacy of slavery affected African-Americans every day.

The book got a lot of attention. Readers praised it, and it even drew the interest of First Lady Eleanor Roosevelt. She suggested that Wright apply for a Guggenheim fellowship. He received that important honor in 1939. It allowed him to devote his time to writing.

NATIVE SON: Wright's next book was *Native Son*. Once again, his theme was the vicious affect of racism on African-American life. The book was a sensation. It tells the story of an African-American, Bigger Thomas, who accidently commits murder and is sentenced to death. The book is an unflinching look at racism in America. In his portrait of Bigger, Wright forced white Americans to look at the reality of the lives of blacks.

Native Son was hugely popular, and controversial, too. **James Baldwin** said that Wright created stereotypes—typical black characters, not real people. **Ralph Ellison** rejected Bigger as a "final image" of an African-American. But he admired Wright's achievement. A major white critic, Irving Howe, said the book "changed American culture forever."

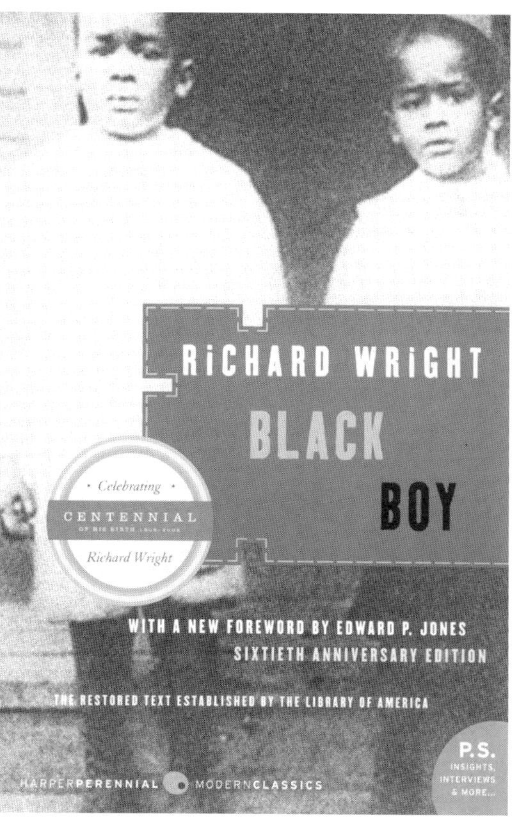

BLACK BOY: Wright's next major book was *Black Boy.* It was his autobiography. He is blunt about how racism, poverty, and hunger fueled his anger at injustice in America. He reveals the way racism defines all aspects of life for African-Americans. Like *Native Son*, *Black Boy* was a sensation. It sold millions of copies. More importantly, it got people, black and white, talking about race.

MOVING TO FRANCE: Around this time, Wright visited France for the first time. He loved the country, and felt welcome there. He decided to move to France permanently. There, he continued to write, and also to teach and give speeches.

Wright also visited many African nations. He wanted to study the history and culture of the continent. He spent the last years of his life writing and traveling. Richard Wright died of a heart attack on November 28, 1960, in Paris. He was 52 years old.

RICHARD WRIGHT'S HOME AND FAMILY: Wright was married twice. His first wife was Dhiman Rose Meadman. They married in 1939 and divorced after two years. In 1941, Wright married Ellen Poplar. They had two daughters, Julia and Rachel.

HIS LEGACY: Wright is remembered for his powerful descriptions of racism in America. His works showed Americans, black and white, the painful truth about how racism ruined lives. His purpose was to expose "the secret black, hidden core of race relations in the United States. Nobody is ever expected to speak honestly about the problem." Richard Wright inspired a dialog that continues to this day.

WORLD WIDE WEB SITES:

http://www.itvs.org/richardwright/
http://www.olemiss.edu/depts/english/ms-riters/dir/wright_richard/

Photo and Illustration Credits

Every effort has been made to trace copyright for the images used in this volume. Any omissions will be corrected in future editions.

Alvin Ailey: Courtesy of the Library of Congress; AP Images.
Marian Anderson: Courtesy of the Library of Congress;
Maya Angelou: Photo: Random House. Covers: KOFI AND HIS MAGIC (Crown Publishers) copyright © 1996 by Maya Angelou and Margaret Courtney-Clarke; MY PAINTED HOUSE, MY CHICKEN AND ME (Crown Publishers) copyright © 1994 by Maya Angelou. Photographs copyright © 1994 by Margaret Courtney-Clarke; MAYA'S WORLD : ANGELINA OF ITALY (a Random House PictureBack Book/Random House) Text copyright © 2004 by Maya Angelou. Illustrations copyright © 2004 by Lizzy Rockwell.
Louis Armstrong: AP Images
James Baldwin: Courtesy of the Library of Congress; GO TELL IT ON THE MOUNTAIN copyright © 1953 by James Baldwin; THE FIRE NEXT TIME copyright © 1962 by James Baldwin.
Romare Bearden: Courtesy of the Library of Congress; Art copyright © Romare Bearden/Licensed by VAGA, New York.
Halle Berry: AP Images; Harpo Films.
Ray Charles: AP Images
Bill Cosby: AP Images
Christopher Paul Curtis: Photo: Tim Keating. Covers: THE WATSONS GO TO BIRMINGHAM—1963 copyright © 1995 by Christopher Paul Curtis; BUD, NOT BUDDY copyright © 1999 by Christopher Paul Curtis; ELIJAH OF BUXTON copyright © 2007 by Christopher Paul Curtis.
Miles Davis: AP Images; BIRTH OF THE COOL/Photo: Aram Avakian.
Ossie Davis: Courtesy of the Library of Congress; 40 Acres and a Mule Filmworks/Universal City Studios; Newscom.com.
Ruby Dee: Courtesy of the Library of Congress; 40 Acres and a Mule Filmworks/Universal City Studios;
Paul Laurence Dunbar: Courtesy of the Library of Congress; LYRICS OF LOWLY LIFE copyright © 1896 by Paul Laurence Dunbar.
Duke Ellington: Courtesy of the Library of Congress; AP Images.
Ralph Ellison: Courtesy of the Library of Congress; INVISIBLE MAN copyright © 1947 by Ralph Ellison.
Ella Fitzgerald: Courtesy of the Library of Congress; AP Images.
Marvin Gaye: AP Images
Savion Glover: AP Images; Copyright © 1991 CTW. Sesame Street Muppets copyright © 1991 Henson.

PHOTO AND ILLUSTRATION CREDITS

Berry Gordy Jr.: AP Images
Alex Haley: AP Images; ROOTS copyright © 1974 by Alex Haley.
Virginia Hamilton: Photo: Ron Rovtar. Covers: THE PEOPLE COULD FLY by Virginia Hamilton. Cover art copyright © 1985 by Leo and Diane Dillon. HER STORIES; A RING OF TRICKSTERS courtesy of Scholastic.
Lorraine Hansberry: AP Images; Columbia Pictures.
Langston Hughes: Courtesy of the Library of Congress; THE DREAM KEEPER AND OTHER POEMS text copyright © 1932 by Alfred A. Knopf; renewed 1960 by Langston Hughes; illustrations copyright 1994 by Brian Pinkney. POETRY FOR YOUNG PEOPLE copyright © 1994 by the Estate of Langston Hughes. Artwork © 2006 by Benny Andrews.
Zora Neale Hurston: Courtesy of the Library of Congress; THEIR EYES WERE WATCHING GOD copyright © 1937 by Zora Neale Hurston; THE THREE WITCHES Text copyright © 2006 by Zora Neale Hurston Trust. Illustrations copyright © 2006 by Faith Ringgold. Adapter's copyright © 2006 Joyce Carol Thomas.
Judith Jamison: Photo/Courtesy Alvin Ailey American Dance Theater; AP Images
Jacob Lawrence: Courtesy of the Library of Congress; HARRIET AND THE PROMISED LAND copyright © 1968, 1993 by Jacob Lawrence. THE GREAT MIGRATION cover art by Jadob Lawrence, © 1993 by The Museum of Modern Art, New York, and The Phillips Collection Cover © 1995 by HarperCollins Publishers.
Spike Lee: Newscom.com; Photo credit: Anthony Barboza; Photo credit: David Lee/Warner Brothers. Photo credit: Charlie Varley/courtesy HBO for image 624812_22july-113.jpg
Wynton Marsalis: AP Images; Joe Sinnott/WNET.
Toni Morrison: Photo: Courtesy Houghton Mifflin Company; BELOVED copyright © 1987, 2004 by Toni Morrison; REMEMBER: THE JOURNEY TO SCHOOL INTEGRATION copyright © 2004 by Toni Morrison.
Walter Dean Myers: Photo: John Craig. HARLEM and THE DRAGON TAKES A WIFE courtesy Scholastic, Inc. THE BLUES OF FLATS BROWN courtesy of Holiday House.
Gordon Parks: Courtesy Ronald Reagan Library; Courtesy of the Library of Congress; Cover: THE LEARNING TREE copyright © 1963 by Gordon Parks.
Jerry Pinkney: Photo: Myles Pinkney. MIRANDY AND BROTHER WIND text copyright © 1988 by Patricia C. McKissack. Illustrations copyright © 1988 by Jerry Pinkney; THE PATCHWORK QUILT text copyright © 1985 by Valerie Flournoy. Pictures copyright © 1985 by Jerry Pinkney; THE TALKING EGGS text copyright © 1989 by Robert D. Sans Souci. Pictures copyright © 1989 by Jerry Pinkney.
Sidney Poitier: AP Images
Paul Robeson: Courtesy of the Library of Congress
Bill "Bojangles" Robinson: Courtesy of the Library of Congress
Madam C. J. Walker: Courtesy of the Library of Congress
Denzel Washington: AP Images; TRISTAR Pictures; Photo: Tracy Bennett; Photo credit: Clive Coote; Photo credit: David Lee/Warner Bros.;
Phillis Wheatley: Courtesy of the Library of Congress; PHILLIS WHEATLEY: COMPLETE WRITINGS, published by Penguin Books, 2001
Oprah Winfrey: Newscom.com
Richard Wright: Courtesy of the Library of Congress; NATIVE SON copyright © 1940 by Richard Wright; BLACK BOY copyright © 1944, 1945 by Richard Wright.

Glossary and Brief Biographies

The Glossary contains terms used in the entries on African-American Leaders. It includes descriptions and definitions of concepts relating to African-American history and culture.

The "Brief Biographies" section includes short profiles of people important to African-American history who do not have full entries in the volume. Glossary terms are capitalized and bold-faced in the entries.

ABOLITION, ABOLITIONIST: The abolitionist movement began in the 1780s in the United States and Europe. Abolitionists wanted to "abolish," or end, slavery, as well as the slave trade. In the 1830s, William Lloyd Garrison started the American Anti-Slavery Society. He called for the freeing of all slaves throughout the nation. Frederick Douglass was an early an ardent advocate of abolition, as were Sojourner Truth and Harriet Tubman.

BROWN V. THE BOARD OF EDUCATION: In 1954, Thurgood Marshall was one of the **NAACP** attorneys in a case called "Brown v. Board of Education of Topeka." (Legal cases are named for the two sides in the suit. In this case, Marshall and the NAACP represented Oliver Brown against the Topeka, Kansas Board of Education.)

At that time, 17 states and the District of Columbia had laws that segregated schools. In the north, states left the decision up to individual school districts. In Topeka, Kansas, schools were legally segregated. All over the country, black children went to schools where buildings were crumbling and books were scarce. The states could *legally* spend more on white students, their teachers, and their facilities than they could for blacks.

Oliver Brown was the father of seven-year-old Linda Brown. He filed the suit on Linda's behalf. Linda had to travel 1 hour 20 minutes to get to her segregated school each day. The school was 21 blocks from her home. She had to cross a dangerous railroad yard every day to get to the bus. Linda's white neighbors walked to a whites-only school that was just 7 blocks from her home. Her father claimed that such treatment was unconstitutional.

The new Chief Justice of the Supreme Court was named Earl Warren. He listened to the Brown case as argued by Marshall. He wrote the Court's response. He agreed with Marshall's argument. He called education "perhaps the most important function of state and local government." He also wrote:

"Does segregation of children in the public schools solely on the basis of race deprive the children of the minority group of equal educational opportunity? We believe it does."

"In the field of education, the doctrine of 'separate but equal' has no place. Separated education facilities are inherently unequal."

With that decision, the Supreme Court declared segregation unconstitutional. It took many years to integrate the public schools, but the Brown decision marked the end of legal discrimination based on race. It was one of the most important decisions of the century. It led to the end of legal segregation in all public facilities.

However, the movement for the integration of the public schools had more obstacles to overcome. In the years following the Brown decision, attempts to integrate public schools met with entrenched resistance and more racial violence. As the case of the Little Rock Nine indicates, it took years, and governmental intervention, to begin to implement integration.

CIVIL RIGHTS ACT: In 1964, the U.S. Congress passed legislation called the Civil Rights Act. It prohibits discrimination based on race, color, religion, or national origin in all public places, including schools, restaurants, hotels, and theaters.

CIVIL RIGHTS MOVEMENT: The term Civil Rights Movement refers to the political and social movement that began in the early 20th century to win equal rights for African-Americans. The movement was spearheaded by such leaders as W.E.B. Du Bois, Ralph Bunche, and Ida B. Wells, working with the **NAACP**. In the 1950s and 1960s, Martin Luther King Jr. led the movement to its greatest legislative achievement, the passage of the **CIVIL RIGHTS ACT** of 1964. That landmark law prohibited discrimination based on race, color, religion, or national origin in all public places, including schools, restaurants, hotels, and theaters. The Voting Rights Act of 1965 guaranteed free access to voting for all Americans. In addition to new laws, a major Supreme Court case furthered the cause of the movement. **BROWN VS. THE BOARD OF EDUCATION** was a case brought by Thurgood Marshall and the **NAACP** against the public schools of Topeka, Kansas. In that landmark decision, the Court ruled that segregation in the public schools was unconstitutional. (See entries on Du Bois, Bunche, Wells, King, and Marshall in *Biography for Beginners: African-American Leaders, Vol. 1.*)

HARLEM RENAISSANCE: In the 1920s, a group of African-American artists—authors, artists, actors, and musicians—settled in the Harlem section of New York. They were devoted to celebrating the African-American experience in their art. Famous artists of the Harlem Renaissance include **ROMARE BEARDEN, JACOB LAWRENCE, DUKE ELLINGTON, RALPH ELLISON,** and **LANGSTON HUGHES.**

JIM CROW: After the Civil War and the passage of the Thirteenth, Fourteenth and Fifteenth Amendments, black Americans thought their hard-fought, new-won rights were guaranteed. The Thirteenth Amendment banned slavery. The Fourteenth Amendment guaranteed the right of full citizenship to African-Americans. The Fifteenth Amendment guaranteed the rights of all citizens, regardless of race, to vote.

Yet the truth of the lives of black Americans was much different. Throughout the country, particularly in the South, blacks had few if any rights. Facilities were segregated by race. Education and jobs were denied them. A series of court cases, especially **BROWN V. THE BOARD OF EDUCATION** as well as the passage of the **CIVIL RIGHTS ACT** helped end Jim Crow and segregation.

NAACP/NATIONAL ASSOCIATION FOR THE ADVANCEMENT OF COLORED PEOPLE: The National Association for the Advancement of Colored People was formed in 1909 in response to the continuing problems of racial injustice in America. Its early leaders included W.E.B. DuBois, Ida B. Wells, Ralph Bunche, and Thurgood Marshall.(See entries on Du Bois, Wells, Bunche, and Marshall in *Biography for Beginners: African-American Leaders, Volume 1.*)

SLAVERY: Slavery is when one person is able to hold or own another person against their will. The slave has no rights and is forced to do whatever work the slave master requires.

Slavery in the New World began shortly after the arrival of the European explorers in the 1500s. The explorers captured and enslaved Native American peoples. The enslavement of African blacks began in Virginia in the 1600s. Traders from Europe captured African people who lived on the west coast of Africa. Then the European traders brought the Africans as slaves to settlements along the Atlantic coast. These settlements later became the colonies of the United States.

People in the U.S. disagreed and argued over slavery from the time of the nation's founding. By the early 1800s most Northern states were enacting laws to end slavery. Some Northerners despised slavery so much that they wanted to "abolish" it, or do away with it. Those were the "**ABOLITIONISTS"** (see above).

But in the South, slaves had worked on plantations since the time of the first settlers. Slaves became especially important to raising crops on the plantations. They did much of the work that earned the money for their white owners. The system of slavery was part of life for white Southerners. Despite its inhumane treatment of black people, the South wanted to keep slavery. And they wanted to extend it.

In the 1800s, the nation was growing as new territories were added in the West. Settlers from the North and South moved into these territories. They disagreed over whether there should be slavery in those new areas. In the 1850s the U.S. Congress tried to work out compromises that would satisfy both the North and the South. The compromises didn't work.

Abraham Lincoln was elected President in 1860. He opposed slavery and wanted to abolish it. After Lincoln's election, eleven Southern states "seceded"—left—the Union. They formed their own separate country, called the Confederate States of America, or the Confederacy. That led to the Civil War, which lasted from 1861 to 1865. In 1863, President Lincoln issued the "Emancipation Proclamation," which freed the slaves. Two years later, in 1865, the North won the war, and the South surrendered. The Confederate states once again became part of the United States, and all the slaves throughout the country were freed.

UNDERGROUND RAILROAD: A secret network of roads and safe houses used by runaway slaves. Traveling at night, they escaped the South and found safety and freedom in the North. The "rail-road" led all the way to northern New York, Michigan, and into Canada. Harriet Tubman was the most famous "conductor" of the Underground Railroad. She brought hundreds of slaves to freedom. (You can read a profile of Tubman in *Biography for Beginners: African-American Leaders, Vol. 1.*)

VOTING RIGHTS ACT: The Voting Rights Act of 1965 guaranteed free access to voting for all Americans. It ended an era when blacks, especially in the South, faced threats, intimidation, literacy tests, and other tactics in trying to register and to vote.

* * *

BRIEF BIOGRAPHIES

BASIE, COUNT: Basie (1904 - 1984) was a jazz pianist and bandleader. Along with **DUKE ELLINGTON** and **LOUIS ARMSTRONG,** he led one of the greatest of the Big Bands. Basie's band was noted for a number of famous jazz soloists, who each added their talent to the group's distinctive "swing" sound and rhythms. Those famous soloists included guitarist Freddie Green, bass player Walter Page, drummer Jo Jones, and Basie on the piano."One O'Clock Jump," and "Jumpin' at the Woodside," are two of his most famous compositions. His recording of "April in Paris" is considered a jazz classic.

BELAFONTE, HARRY: Belafonte (1927 -) is an actor, musician, and activist. He was born in Harlem and moved with his mother to Jamaica when he was a child. He moved back to Harlem and started to perform. He had an award-winning career as an actor, and began a singing career in New York, too. He often sang songs in the Calypso tradition of the West Indies. One of his most famous recordings was of "The Banana Boat Song," known as "Day-O." His success with this and other albums made him one of the most famous "cross-over" artists in popular music. He appeared in many popular films, including *Uptown Saturday Night.* He became the first African-American to win an Emmy for his television special, *Tonight with Belafonte.* He was also committed to the cause of Civil Rights in the U.S., fought against apartheid in South Africa, and raised money to fight world famine.

BROOKS, GWENDOLYN: Brooks (1917 - 2000) was a poet and writer who was the first African-American to win the Pulitzer Prize for poetry. She was influenced by the **HARLEM RENAISSANCE** poet **Lansgton Hughes**, and, like him, wrote poems that celebrated the African-American experience. One of her most famous early works was *Annie Allen*. The book's poems center on a young black girl growing up. *Annie Allen* won the Pulitzer Prize, one of the most important awards for writers. Brooks was the first African-American to receive a Pulitzer. She was also influenced by the Black Arts Movement. They believed that "black poets should write as blacks, about blacks, and address themselves to blacks." The movement inspired some of her greatest works, including *In the Mecca* and *Riot*. She was also devoted to spreading the influence of poetry. She was named the Poetry Consultant to the Library of Congress in 1985. She was the first African-American woman to achieve that important award.

GILLESPIE, DIZZY: Gillespie (1917 - 1993) was a jazz trumpeter and composer. His name when he was born was John Birks Gillespie. He got the nickname "Dizzy" later. He started his career in a "swing" band, which played a type of jazz music popular in the 1930s and 1940s that had a steady beat, a distinct melody, and simple harmonies. From the time he first began to play, Dizzy liked to take the melody apart, to rearrange chords, and to explore the harmonies and rhythms he heard in the music. Dizzy was on his way to creating the type of jazz—bebop—with which his name became linked and which made him famous. In 1939, Gillespie met **CHARLIE PARKER**. Known as "Yardbird," Parker was an alto saxophonist whose name is also linked to the birth of bebop. Unlike the swing style of jazz played by the big bands, bebop was music to listen to, not to dance to. Its complex chords were too unusual for some who were used to the easy harmonies of swing. Improvisation has always been a part of jazz, but even in this area bebop offered something new. Bebop explored the harmonic qualities, especially the chord progressions, rather than the melodic possibilities of a piece. Gillespie was a lifelong experimenter with music, making recordings of Afro-Cuban and other musical styles until his death.

HOLIDAY, BILLIE: Holiday (1915 - 1959) was one of the leading jazz and blues singers of the 20th century. Known as "Lady Day," her name when she was born was Eleanora Fagan. She began her career singing in Harlem nightclubs and performed with some of the major jazz bands, including **COUNT BASIE** (see above). She had a career as a vocalist singing with bands, and as a soloist. Holiday was known as a superb interpreter of songs. Her recording of "Strange Fruit," about a lynching, is considered a masterpiece. Sadly, Holiday was addicted to heroin, and her outstanding career was cut short by her addiction. She died at the age of 44. Her autobiography, *Lady Sings the Blues*, was the basis of a 1972 film that starred **DIANA ROSS** as Holiday.

JONES, JAMES EARL: Jones (1931 -) is one of the finest American actors of his generation. He has had a distinguished career on the stage, starring in New York productions ranging from Shakespeare's *Othello* to *The Great White Hope*. He also starred in a one-man show based on the life of **Paul Robeson**. Jones has appeared in many television shows, including a part in *Roots II*, based on **Alex Haley's** novel. His notable film career includes roles in *Field of Dreams, Dr. Strangelove*, and several Tom Clancey movies. But he is best known to generations of film lovers as the voice of Darth Vader in the *Star Wars* movies, and as the voice of Mufasa in *The Lion King*.

JONES, QUINCY: Jones (1933 -), a musician, composer, arranger, and producer has been at the center of American music for more than 50 years. He played in a band with **Ray Charles** as a teenager.

He helped arrange and produce the music of **Louis Armstong, Count Basie, Miles Davis, Dizzy Gillespie** and **Stevie Wonder**. He wrote the music for **Alex Haley's** *Roots*, and film scores, too. He is best known to current audiences as the producer of Michael Jackson's *Thriller*, one of the best-selling recordings of all time. He also produced "We Are The World," an international hit that raised money for famine relief in 1985. In addition, he started Qwest Communications and *Vibe* magazine, and produced the TV hit, "The Fresh Prince of Bel Air." His influence is still felt throughout the music world.

MONK, THELONIUS: Monk (1917 - 1982) was one of the most important figures in 20th century jazz music. Along with **DIZZY GILLESPIE** and **CHARLIE PARKER**, he was one of the founders of bebop. He had studied classical music in addition to jazz, and he brought that knowledge to the creation of bebop. He wrote several bebop standards, including "Round Midnight," and appeared on many of the greatest jazz recordings with musicians like **Miles Davis.**

PARKER, CHARLIE: Parker (1920 - 1955) was a saxophone player and one of the most important figures in the history of jazz. Known as "Yardbird," or "Bird," he was a colleague of **DIZZY GILLESPIE**, and the two of them, with **THELONIUS MONK**, pioneered the bebop style of jazz. Unlike the swing style of jazz played by the big bands, bebop was music to listen to, not to dance to. Its complex chords were too unusual for some who were used to the easy harmonies of swing. Improvisation has always been a part of jazz, but even in this area bebop offered something new. Bebop explored the harmonic qualities, especially the chord progressions, rather than the melodic possibilities of a piece. Parker played in some of the greatest jazz ensembles of the 20th century, with Gillespie, Monk, **Miles Davis,** Earl Hines, and Billy Eckstine. Sadly, this great musicians life was cut short by his addiction to drugs and alcohol. He died at 34.

ROSS, DIANA: Ross (1944 -) is a singer and actress who got her start at **Berry Gordy**'s Motown. She started off as the lead singer of The Supremes, one of the most successful groups of the modern pop era. The group had a string of Number One hits in the 1960s, including the popular "Baby Love" and "Stop in the Name of Love." Ross went off on her own to begin a successful solo career in the 1970s. She also began to appear in films, starring as **BILLIE HOLIDAY** in 1972's *Lady Sings the Blues.*

VAUGHAN, SARAH: Vaughan (1924 - 1990) was one of the greatest jazz singers of the 20th century. Called "The Divine" and "Sassy," she was noted for her unique ability to bring out the meaning in the music. Whether she was singing classic jazz songs, pop songs, or Broadway tunes, she could improvise around a tune and make it her own. She had a great range, and a powerful technique. Fellow musicians said that she "thought" like a musician, seeing the instrumental possibilities in interpreting a song. Her phrasing—the ability to follow a musical line to give it the most meaning—was widely praised.

WONDER, STEVIE: Wonder (1950 -) is a singer and composer who has been performing since he was a child. His name when he was born was Steveland Morris. He has been blind since he was an infant, and began to play piano at four. First known as "Little Stevie Wonder," he had his first hit with "Fingertips" when he was just 13 years old. Wonder's records were some of the most popular to come out of **Berry Gordy's** Motown. He has always written most of his own music, and has also played all the instruments on his recordings. His many hits over the years include "Ma Cherie Amour," "Signed, Sealed Delivered," and albums *Songs in the Key of Life, Hotter than July* and *Innvervisions.* He also composed the soundtrack to **Spike Lee's** *Jungle Fever.* Wonder is perhaps best known to modern audiences for championing the establishment of a national holiday in honor of Martin Luther King Jr. He led that effort with one of his greatest hits, "Happy Birthday to You." (See the entry on King in *Biography for Beginners: African-American Leaders, Vol. 1.*)

Subject Index

This index contains the names, occupations, and key words relating to the individuals profiled in this volume. It also includes significant historical events covered in the biographical profiles. Bold-faced type indicates the main entry on an individual.